# Factional and Coalition Politics in China

# Y. C. Chang

# Factional and Coalition Politics in China

## The Cultural Revolution and Its Aftermath

PRAEGER SPECIAL STUDIES IN INTERNATIONAL POLITICS AND GOVERNMENT

**Praeger Publishers**   New York   Washington   London

29265

Library of Congress Cataloging in Publication Data

Chang, Yi-Chun, 1932-
    Factional and coalition politics in China.

    (Praeger special studies in international politics
and government)
    Includes bibliographical references.
    1. Communism—China.   2.  China—Politics and
government—1949-        I.  Title.
HX388.5.C48              320.9'51'05        75-8404
ISBN 0-275-00920-3

PRAEGER PUBLISHERS
111 Fourth Avenue, New York, N.Y. 10003, U.S.A.

Published in the United States of America in 1976
by Praeger Publishers, Inc.

Printed in the United States of America

# ACKNOWLEDGMENTS

In the preparation of this book, I owe a great debt to many institutions and individuals. Over the years the University of Delaware has been most generous in giving me financial support at various stages of my work, as well as the opportunity to do research during my sabbatical year in Asia. I also wish to thank the Union Research Institute, Hong Kong; the Graduate School of East Asian Studies, National Chengch'i University; and the Institute of International Relations, Republic of China; for allowing me to use their files. I was thus enabled to gain a deeper understanding of China than otherwise would have been the case.

To the many colleagues and friends in the field of China and other disciplines who helped me in the study of such an elusive topic, I am grateful. Besides those who, for reasons of their own, wish to remain anonymous, I express my gratitude to James C. Hsiung, King C. Chen, Parris H. Chang, Raymond Wolters, Glenn D. Paige, and Kenneth Haas. All read parts of this manuscript and made valuable comments and suggestions; none, of course, agreed with all of my interpretations and analyses. John Merrill performed well beyond the call of duty for a graduate assistant. Lastly, I am thankful to my wife Nina who unstintingly gave her time as editor and even typist day in and day out. Any book dealing with a subject as controversial and imperfectly understood as politics in China cannot be entirely free of errors; for the ones found in this study, I alone am accountable.

# CONTENTS

# LIST OF TABLES

# LIST OF ABBREVIATIONS

| | |
|---|---|
| AR | Autonomous Region |
| ARPC | Autonomous Region Party Committee |
| CC | Central Committee |
| CCP | Chinese Communist Party |
| CCRG | Central Cultural Revolution Group |
| GPCR | Great Proletarian Cultural Revolution |
| MAC | Military Affairs Commission |
| MD | Military District |
| MPC | Municipal Party Committee |
| MR | Military Region |
| NPC | National People's Congress |
| PLA | People's Liberation Army |
| PPC | Provincial Party Committee |
| RC | Revolutionary Committee |

The Cultural Revolution, which shook the very foundation of the Chinese Communist regime, has produced an equally disturbing impact on our study of China. Many central concepts we had previously taken for granted in our analyses have proved to be of questionable usefulness, and many commonly accepted theses have become invalid. In fact, our imperfect understanding of China has been shown for what it is by our inability to explain, much less predict, what has happened in China since 1966. Our hope to gather hard, reliable information when the bamboo curtain was finally lifted for some chosen scholars and scientists was somewhat disappointed; those few privileged to obtain a visa were restricted as to whom they could contact, where they could go, and what kinds of questions they could ask. They returned with amazingly little to enlighten a still confused, puzzled world.

This study was undertaken to make some sense, hopefully, out of the series of seemingly unrelated, perplexing events in China since the Cultural Revolution by utilizing as a focus of analysis the concepts of "faction" and "coalition." The use of the term "faction" in describing and analyzing politics in China has itself been the subject of debate. Some would argue whether there are indeed factions in China, as the term is understood in the West, and whether, assuming their existence, they can be clearly identified. Still others quibble over the precise meaning of the term. To eliminate at the outset any semantic arguments, "faction" is used here as the most appropriate English translation of the Chinese term *p'ai chi,* which, quoting Harold D. Lasswell, means "any constituent group of a larger unit which works for the advancement of particular persons or policies."[1] Factions defined in these terms are often referred to by the Chinese Communists themselves. Mao Tse-tung admitted in his speech to the Eleventh Plenum of the Eighth Central Committee on August 13, 1966:

Do we have a party outside our Party? I think that we do, and that we have factions inside the Party. We used to criticize the Kuomintang, who said: 'No party outside the Party and no factions inside the Party.' Some people put it: 'No party outside the Party is autocracy; no factions inside the Party is nonsense.' This applies to us. You may say that there are no factions in our Party, but there are.[2]

And in a prior speech on March 5, 1959, Mao talked about the presence of "mountain tops" in the army, which again could be interpreted as factions:

Our Party had many 'mountain tops' in the past and we gradually united them to form a unified Party. There were also several 'mountain tops' within our troops. The First Front Army had two 'mountain tops'; the Second Front Army had two; troops in north Shensi had two; the Fourth Front Army had four 'mountain tops.' At the Party School in Yenan, there were 'mountain tops' when students went for a walk after sunset or a meal in the restaurants. If they belonged to the same 'mountain top,' they talked about everything and anything but they were not as free with others. Even when heading for the air-raid shelters in north Shensi, cadres from other areas would not take the same route as the local cadres. They wouldn't mix even when their lives were at stake. What policy should we adopt? We should get to know the 'mountain tops,' recognize them, take care of them, and destroy them.[3]

That such a policy, if it was ever truly implemented, was unsuccessful is suggested by the persistence of factions which gradually evolved into the major contending forces of the Cultural Revolution, as this study attempts to show.

The book begins with an attempt to identify these factional groups and their major policy differences, not only within the broad categories of "Left, Middle, and Right,"[4] as the Chinese Communists define them, but also in terms of factions within factions, although this can be more easily accomplished at the national level than at the provincial and local levels (Chapters 1 and 2). It then describes the "twists and turns" of the Cultural Revolution and analyzes in sequential terms the rise and fall of these groups: How did the People's Liberation Army and Lin Piao become involved in the turmoil, and how did they acquire a dominant role in the Revolutionary Committees at the local level by default (Chapter 3)? How did the Party first attempt to rebuild itself at the national level (Chapter 4) and then at the provincial level (Chapter 5)? Why was Lin Piao purged (Chapter 6) and how did the leftists, in coalition with Chou En-lai, restructure the Party by eliminating Lin's supporters and the military (Chapter 7)? What is the relative strength of the leftists and the emerging group centered around Chou, as revealed by the Fourth National People's Congress, which adopted a new Constitution of the People's Republic (Chapter 8)? The conclusion (Chapter 9) discusses more theoretically factional and coalition politics in China and attempts to forecast in tentative terms the most likely prospects for China in the immediate future.

The Cultural Revolution presents an ideal case for studying factional struggle in China because it was in essence the culmination of festering internal strife dating back to the 1950s. It was also the most widespread conflict in China, involving thousands of Party cadres both in Peking and in the nation's far-flung provinces; and the most violent, for there were hundreds of thousands of casualties, though the exact number may never be known. Finally, we have relatively more information on the Cultural Revolution than on previous controversies. Red Guard publications are widely available in the West, and though some give exaggerated accounts, many are essentially accurate when stripped of political verbiage.[5] Furthermore, many Chinese Communist documents classified as "secret" or "top-secret," which were acquired by Taiwan, have now been made public. For many years, any information released by Taiwan was automatically regarded with suspicion. However, Western authorities on China have belatedly acknowledged the reliability of these documents. Stuart Schram, for one, admitted in his book *Chairman Mao Talks to the People:*

> The remaining three [documents] have been taken from a periodical devoted to Chinese communist affairs published in Taipei. This might appear to render them suspect, but in fact the organizations on Taiwan involved in research on these problems, while free in their speculations regarding events in China, have been exceedingly prudent in reproducing documents, and those they have made available have often been subsequently proved to be authentic.[6]

The present study has made generous use of materials from both sides of the Taiwan Straits.

Given the scarcity of reliable data on China, my attempt here must be considered exploratory and preliminary. Despite the missing links and glaring gaps which abound in this study, the basic arguments of this analysis are, I believe, realistic and sound.

## NOTES

1. Harold D. Lasswell, "Faction," in *Encyclopedia of Social Sciences 6,* eds. Edwin R. A. Seligman and Alvin Johnson (New York: The Macmillan Co., 1931), p. 49.

2. *Mao Tse-tung ssu-hsiang wan-sui (Long Live Mao Tse-tung's Thoughts),* vol. 1, (n. p., 1969), p. 652; also found in *Chairman Mao Talks to the People,* ed. Stuart Schram (New York: Pantheon Books, 1974), p. 263.

3. *Long Live Mao Tse-tung's Thoughts,* vol. 2, op. cit., p. 46.

4. Commentator, "Make a Class Analysis of Factionalism," *Peking Review,* no. 19 (May 10, 1968), p. 3.

5. See, for example, Parris H. Chang, *Power and Policy in China* (University Park, Pa.: Pennsylvania State University Press, 1975), p. 7.

6. Schram, op. cit., pp. 50–51.

# 1

## ORIGINS OF THE
## CULTURAL REVOLUTION:
## THE RIGHTISTS

The Great Proletarian Cultural Revolution, which erupted suddenly and violently in 1966, was actually many years in the making. Its origins were deeply embedded in an ideological dispute regarding the best method for implementing the tenets of Marxism-Leninism in China. As early as 1949, Mao Tse-tung, in an obvious attempt to define correct policy, had proclaimed:

> The general line and over-all responsibility of our Party during this period of transition is to gradually realize, during a considerably lengthy period, the socialization of our industry, agriculture, handcraft enterprises and capitalist commercial [business]. This general line is the lighthouse for our work. To depart from it, no matter what kind of work we undertake, is to commit right or left mistakes.[1]

After Peking consolidated its political rule and embarked on a program of "socialization," ideological differences, which had been kept quiet during the early years of the People's Republic (misleading many Westerners into thinking that the new Communist leadership was cohesive and unified), now manifested themselves in a variety of ways and increasingly became the subject of heated debate. The failure in 1958 of Mao's policy of "Three Red Banners" brought this issue into sharper focus and in fact raised the question of who had committed "right or left mistakes." Many Party leaders and top bureaucrats, not wishing to publicly oppose Mao, voiced their dissenting opinions within the Party. The leader of this group was Liu Shao-ch'i, then chairman of the People's Republic, who had been Mao's hand-picked heir chosen at the Seventh Party Congress in 1945.

# THE TWO ROADS TO SOCIALISM: LIU SHAO-CH'I VERSUS MAO TSE-TUNG

As far back as 1939, Mao and Liu had differed over what was the most direct road to socialism, primarily because of their differing revolutionary experiences. Mao's preference for an agrarian, peasant-oriented communism is well known. Liu, on the other hand, subscribing to the orthodox Leninist view and having close ties with the urban labor movement, regarded the peasants as an auxiliary force to the workers, who should "take them by the hand" and lead them.[2] He was constantly concerned with Party structure and discipline, which he regarded as the key to a successful revolutionary movement. More importantly, Liu emphasized the Party as the source of authority in a Communist society, in contrast to Mao's intensely more personalized concept of leadership.[3] Nevertheless, Liu, then a loyal and enthusiastic supporter of Mao, praised Mao, in his "Report Concerning the Revision of the Party Constitution" given at the Seventh Party Congress (1945), as the greatest revolutionary and theoretician in all of Chinese history, and labeled his thoughts "the highest expression of the wisdom of the Chinese nation."[4] However, with the civil war won and the reconstruction of China underway, the disagreement between Mao and Liu deepened and extended into many related issues.

## Personality Cult

The de-Stalinization campaign that began at the Twentieth Soviet Party Congress in February 1956 had a profound impact on the Chinese Communist Party (CCP). At the Eighth Party Congress (of the CCP) in September 1956, Liu stressed in his "Political Report" that the Soviet Union had criticized the phenomenon of the "personality cult" for inflicting serious damage on the Soviet Communist Party. Liu urged that the Chinese Communist Party at every level implement the principle of "collective leadership" without exception. Teng Hsiao-p'ing, then secretary general of the Party, sided with Liu and declared in his "Report Concerning the Revision of the Party Constitution":

> Our Party is also tired of individual deification. . . . Our duty is to oppose sternly 'the singling out of the individual' and the adulation of the individual.[5]

And he noted further:

> There are still many shortcomings in the implementation of 'collective leadership' in the Party. A small minority of Party leaders still exhibit the

inclination of 'individual monopoly'. . . . We must oppose those who practice the substance of 'individual monopoly' under the pretence of 'collective leadership.'[6]

Liu, who first coined the expression "Mao Tse-tung's Thought" in his 1943 article entitled "Liquidate Menshevist Ideology in the Party"[7] and who once said that the "thoughts of Mao is Chinese Marxism,"[8] welcomed a suggestion made by P'eng Teh-huai, then minister of defense, to delete from the 1956 Party Constitution the provision in the 1945 Party Constitution (ratified by the Seventh Party Congress) that had proclaimed:

The Chinese Communist Party is guided in all its works by the 'thought of Mao Tse-tung,' which is the unification of the Marxist-Leninist theory with the experience of the Chinese revolution.[9]

Thus, the 1956 Party Constitution, though retaining the provision that "Marxism-Leninism is the guideline for action,"[10] omitted all reference to the thoughts of Mao Tse-tung. In addition, it created the position of "honorary chairman" in anticipation of Mao's early retirement.

## THE COLLECTIVIZATION OF AGRICULTURE AND THE GREAT LEAP FORWARD

For a basically agrarian country like China, managing the agricultural sector is a concern of the highest priority. Mao felt that, after the completion of land reform, steps needed to be taken immediately to socialize agriculture by pursuing a policy of collectivization. Liu had always linked collectivization to the progress of mechanization or the availability of agricultural machinery,[11] and viewed Mao's policies as too "ambitious" and "adventurous," claiming that "the experience of cadres" and "the awareness of the masses" did not permit rapid expansion of the commune program. He advocated the adoption of more moderate measures, even urging some peasants to withdraw from elementary cooperatives, thus undermining, it was charged, Mao's policy of collectivization in the mid-1950s.[12]

Ridiculing Liu as a "woman with bound feet" who complained that others were walking too fast, Mao retorted:

There are people who remain in the same place after the completion of the 'democratic revolution.' They do not understand changes of a revolutionary nature, continue to implement 'new democracy,' do nothing to further socialism, and therefore commit mistakes of the right.[13]

On balance, the First Five-Year Plan, copying that of the Soviet Union, had been highly successful, but Mao and the Party leadership were increasingly aware of the inapplicability of the Soviet model to China. By 1957 Soviet development loans had been almost completely exhausted, and the prospect of more long-term Russian credits was remote. The fragile economy was further taxed by a balance-of-payments problem resulting from repaying past Soviet loans. Moreover, there were internal problems particularly disturbing to Mao, such as the great power wielded by an ever-growing economic bureaucracy, a decreased emphasis on revolutionary values, and a persistent neglect of the role of the masses.[14] In the face of this deteriorating situation, Mao proposed his Three Red Banners campaign which was enthusiastically endorsed by the Second Session of the Eighth Party Congress in May 1958. To accomplish its objectives, Mao proposed to "walk on two legs"—to increase growth in the agricultural and industrial sectors using both modern capital-intensive and indigenous labor-intensive methods. As a means of utilizing the country's huge manpower pool most effectively and encouraging local self-sufficiency, Mao argued for the decentralization of economic planning and management to give greater discretion to provincial Party authorities and, typically, to substitute political indoctrination for material incentives.

By merging the advanced agricultural production cooperatives, communes were created as early as April 1958 in parts of Honan province. Most regions had established some variety of this new agricultural form by midsummer, and the Politburo of the Central Committee (CC) proclaimed at the Peitaiho Conference of August 17, 1958, that the creation of communes was the "basic policy of the Party" and their establishment would be obligatory.

The high level of enthusiasm displayed at Peitaiho rapidly cooled by November 1958. The nation's agricultural and industrial production had shown a marked decline; and growing discontent among the masses had brought about widespread disorder, alerting Liu and other top Party leaders to the potential threats to the very foundations of the Communist regime. Liu called for a series of conferences to consider some readjustments in the policies of the "Three Red Banners." The first of these conferences was held in Chengchou, Honan, from November 2 to 10, 1958; after much heated debate, the meeting ended in a deadlock between the Party Central and leading local cadres who had become the target of attack by peasants for administering such an unpopular program. Another conference, immediately preceding the Sixth Plenum of the Eighth CC, was convened in Wuhan, but again failed to obtain support of the first secretaries of the Provincial Party Committees (PPC) who attended.

At the Sixth Plenum in Wuhan on November 28, 1958, the Liuists voiced for the first time some of their doubts and reservations regarding the Great Leap, as Ch'en Po-ta, Mao's personal secretary, openly acknowledged:

Regarding our total mobilization in industrial production some say 'it is very
good,' while others say 'it is very bad'. . . .
They regarded this movement as having disturbed the order of production, destroyed the proper balance, created tension and resulted in more loss
than gain. In other words, they felt that only total chaos came out of this
movement. . . .[15]

Yen Ta-kai, then Party secretary from Hopei, echoed Ch'en by noting
that "there are people who claimed that we have leaped to the ceiling and
should leap no more" and that this policy was too adventurous and bound to
fail since "no one has tried it before now or earlier, here or abroad."[16]

Liu's criticism of the commune program, revealed many years later,
centered around his contention that the communes were supported by a minority who ignored the objective, materialistic foundation for such development;
that the establishment of the communes, differing little from the more advanced agricultural cooperatives, was redundant, and that "it was too premature, too fast and would turn sour."[17]

In a spirit of compromise, the "Resolution Regarding Many Questions
Related to the People's Communes" was passed at the Sixth Plenum; it con-
ceded that a "considerable length of time" would be needed to complete
collectivization in the villages, and as a mild rebuke to Mao, went on to say:

They are good-hearted people in our own ranks, but they are over-eager.
They think that the building of a highly developed modern industry and so
on, full realization of socialist ownership by the whole people, or even
attainment of communism, are very easy things. They think that ownership
in the rural people's communes is even now of the nature of ownership by
the whole people and that very soon or even now they can dispense with the
socialist principle of 'to each according to his work' and adopt the communist principle of 'to each according to his needs.' Consequently, they cannot
understand why the socialist system will have to continue for a very long
time. Their view, of course, is a misconception, which must be cleared up.[18]

This resolution, still declaring the people's communes as a "step forward," modified many of their unpalatable aspects. Thus, the people's commune movement in the cities was temporarily interrupted, and a
reinvestigation of all communes begun. Private ownership of houses, vegeta-
bles gardens, and small animals was guaranteed "for all time"; bank deposits
were returned; the eight-hour day, cash wages, and voluntary use of commune
nurseries and canteens were recommended, and the principle of reward according to the amount of work performed accepted.

The Sixth Plenum also approved the "wish of Comrade Mao Tse-tung not
to stand again as a candidate for the Chairmanship of the People's Republic
after the end of his term in office,"[19] thereby permitting him to undertake his

favorite pursuit—philosophical and theoretical study of policies or, in his own words, the "second line"—and to delegate the actual administration of policies to China's other top bureaucratic leaders in the Party and government. Liu Shao-ch'i then was elected Mao's successor as state chairman at the first plenary session of the Second National People's Congress on April 27, 1959.

## Opposition to the "Three Red Banners" and P'eng Teh-huai

Despite these accelerated efforts to remedy the situation, conditions in the communes continued to worsen. There was chaos in the villages and the bankruptcy of the agricultural economy seemed imminent. As a result, sentiment grew even among the central Party leadership to oppose the Great Leap Forward and the communes. Among this opposition, the group led by P'eng Teh-huai was particularly critical and tenacious, and the internal disagreements reached a climax at a stormy six-week succession of conferences at Lushan, Kiangsi—an enlarged session of the Politburo held from July 2 to August 1, 1959, followed by the Eighth Plenum of the Eighth CC from August 2 to 16. From the beginning of the sessions, Mao's critics, led by P'eng, "launched a ferocious attack"[20] on the chairman. In an "Open Letter" to Mao on July 14, 1959, P'eng drew attention to some of the more glaring defects of the "Three Red Banners" program. He pointed out that "some projects for capital construction in 1958 were too hasty or excessive";[21] "some resources [material and financial] and manpower were wasted";[22] and that "the habit of exaggeration [in reporting grain output] . . . spread rather universally," while "there are still a number of people who do not have enough to eat."[23] These "Left" mistakes, according to P'eng, resulted from "petty-bourgeoisie fanaticism":[24]

> We forgot the mass line and the style of seeking truth from facts which the Party had formed over a long time. So far as our method of thinking was concerned, we often confused strategic planning with concrete measures, the long-term policies with immediate steps, the whole truth with the part, and the big collective with the small collective.[25]

More pointedly, P'eng argued:

> In the view of some comrades, putting politics in command could be a substitute for everything. . . . Putting politics in command is no substitute for the economic principles, still less for the concrete measures in economic work.[26]

If later reports are accurate, what actually took place was far more heated and acrimonious than P'eng's "Open Letter" would indicate.[27] P'eng wrote, for example, that the Great Leap was a "rush of blood to the brain" and a "high fever"; that the communes were created prematurely and were "a mess"; that if "the Chinese workers and peasants were not as good as they are," a "Hungarian incident" would have happened in China, and "it would have been necessary to invite Soviet troops in."[28]

In a 40-minute reply on July 23, 1959, Mao refuted P'eng's accusations:

> P'eng Te[h]-huai's letter is of the nature of a program and opposes our general line. . . . He describes the refining of steel by the millions upon millions of people as bourgeois fanaticism and says that the tendency to exaggerate things prevails in all departments all over the country. He actually wants to abolish the people's communes.[29]

Even P'eng's self-effacing remark that he was "crude" and had "no tact"[30] did not escape Mao, who scornfully said that P'eng is "quite subtle. We talk about gains and losses, but he talks about losses and gains, putting losses in the first place."[31]

In any event, Mao, having initially accepted criticism of his program as inevitable, lashed back at his enemies at the session "with tears in his eyes" and threatened an open Party split:

> If we deserve to perish I shall go away, I shall go to the countryside and lead the peasants to overthrow the government. If you of the People's Liberation Army [PLA] will not follow me, then I shall find a Red Army. But I believe that the People's Liberation Army will follow me.[32]

At this point the generals present each got up in turn and pledged their loyalty to Mao and the CC,[33] and Mao succeeded in mustering support in his move to condemn P'eng as antiparty, for while Liu and his followers favored extensive revision of Mao's policies, they were not willing to defy him.

P'eng was dismissed from his post as minister of defense on September 17, 1959, and Lin Piao, who was to create Mao's "Red Army," succeeded P'eng. Huang K'o-ch'eng, P'eng's chief of staff, was implicated and disgraced. Chang Wen-tien and Wang Chia-hsiang, both vice-ministers of the Ministry of Foreign Affairs and intimately connected with P'eng, were purged, and in turn their close associates met a similar fate.[34]

## Dismantlement of the Great Leap and the People's Communes

Despite Mao's emotional outburst and open threat, the Eighth Plenum of the Eighth CC met, reviewed thoroughly the difficulties of the Great Leap, and made three far-reaching decisions. First, the principle of "three layers of control" of commune products was introduced:

> Ownership at the production brigade level constitutes the basic one. Ownership at the commune level constitutes another part. A small part of the ownership should also be vested in the production team.[35]

Second, the earlier principle of "centralized control and divided management"[36] was modified to that of "divided management and divided accounting," suggesting that units of production should be individually responsible for their own performance. Third, the principle of reward according to labor performed that had been first put forth at the Sixth Plenum was reiterated.

A secret report called the "Twelve Regulations," issued by the CC in November of 1960, represented a large-scale retreat, from earlier, more ambitious plans. Among the measures to correct the excesses of the collectivization campaign, the most important were the decisions to permit the peasants to cultivate small "private lots" and engage in family "secondary" enterprise on a small scale, and to revive village fairs and markets.

To reiterate his earlier convictions, Liu Shao-ch'i in blunt terms told the 7,000 cadres attending an enlarged work conference of the CC in Peking on January 26, 1962:

> How did such a difficult situation appear? Why was it that production of food, cloth and consumer goods was not increased but decreased? What is the reason? One is natural disasters. . . . The other is that since 1958 we have had shortcomings and mistakes in our work. I went to a place in Hunan. There the peasants said that 30 percent of the difficulties were brought about by natural calamities, while 70 percent were caused by man-made factors. This you will have to admit.[37]

The participants at this meeting also heard Mao, while delivering a strong self-criticism, still defend his policies even in the face of persuasive evidence presented by Liu and derived from a study clandestinely prepared by P'eng Chen, mayor of Peking and close associate of Liu, in a plot known as the "Ch'ang Kuan Lou Incident."

If these later charges are true, P'eng, with the support of Liu Shao-ch'i,[38] initiated his attack on Mao's "Three Red Banners" in early 1961 by sending investigative teams to various parts of the country under the pretext of "visiting relatives" to gather incriminating material. P'eng then summoned members of his clique to Ch'ang Kuan Lou in the Peking Zoo, in December of the same year, where they spent nine days poring over documents issued by Mao without the approval of the CC to Party organizations at the *hsien* level and above during the period 1958–61, and compiled the "Excerpts of the Central

Committee's Documents," a 20,000-word report listing Mao's 29 "crimes" in such fields as agriculture, industry, finance, trade, and education.

The report cited 110 examples to support the group's contentions that the commune program was implemented prematurely and was beyond the political consciousness of China's peasants:

> The policy of achieving greater, faster, better and more economical results is full of contradictions. If you want to have greater and faster results, you can't have better and more economical results. Rome was not built in a day.[39]

Criticism of Mao was even bolder in the report's footnotes, for he was described as "conceited," "dizzy with victory," and one who wished "to be the first to enter Communism."[40] The study concluded that "our economy is on the verge of bankruptcy and it may not recover in seven or eight years."[41]

P'eng's "black gang," as later information described it, numbered more than a dozen men. Teng T'o, editor of *People's Daily* until 1959 and secretary of the Peking Municipal Party Committee (MPC), assumed "the responsibility of providing guidance"[42] at P'eng's request. The "No. 2 leader," Liu Jen, dispatched the investigative teams to the countryside, and the "No. 3 leader," Cheng T'ian-hsiang, praised the report for having uncovered many problems.[43] Hsiang Tzu-ming, who handled the plot's organizational details, claimed that the communes were "set up at sudden impulse," and dismissed the Great Leap as "high-sounding talk."[44] Lu Yü, Wan I, Sung Ju-fen, and Sung Shuo similarly ridiculed the aims and accomplishments of the Great Leap. Sung Shuo declared that Mao's policies had "damaged the strength of the state" and "caused inflation," and blamed Mao for having "gone too far."[45]

The Liuists continued their offensive during the West Chamber Conference, an enlarged session of the Standing Committee of the Politburo, which convened in February 1962. Overtly cautious, Liu said, without mentioning names:

> A Party member, no matter how capable he is . . . however great the role he plays in the Party, is one element in the apparatus. . . . He should lead and impel the whole Party from within and should not lead the Party from without or above. Democratic centralism within the Party is not who leads whom, but collective leadership. Everyone should . . . submit to the majority. In our Party there are no personal privileges. Unless in the name of the organization, no one is allowed to lead.[46]

In May 1962, Liu won a substantial victory when the "Sixty Articles" was promulgated, giving birth to the slogan "Three Freedoms-One Guarantee,"[47] a popularization of the three newly granted privileges of private plots of land, free markets, and a liberalized policy of free enterprise, with each household responsible for meeting its production quota set by the state. Liu had succeeded in modifying China's economic policies to the extent that the commune program in effect was literally abandoned. In the summer of 1962 Liu even began an effort to rehabilitate "Right deviationists" who had been reprimanded in the autumn of 1959. P'eng Teh-huai, after undergoing "labor reform," was encouraged by Liu and P'eng Chen to refute the charges made earlier against him at the Lushan Plenum.

## Mao's Counterattack and the Socialist Education Movement

Taking the offensive during the Tenth Plenum of the Eighth CC in September 1962, Mao expressed his indignation at the "erroneous tendencies" so flagrantly shown by Liu Shao-ch'i and reminded the people to "never forget class struggle":

> [T]here still exist in society bourgeois influence, the force of habit of old society and the spontaneous tendency toward capitalism among part of the small producers. Therefore, among the people, a small number of persons, making up only a tiny fraction of the total population, who have not yet undergone socialist remoulding, always attempt to depart from the socialist road and turn to the capitalist road whenever there is an opportunity. . . . [W]e must remain vigilant and resolutely oppose in good time various opportunistic ideological tendencies in the Party.[48]

At this plenary session P'eng Teh-huai submitted his report of over 80,000 words, "two years"[49] in preparation, which repeated his earlier criticisms of the "Three Red Banners."[50] At the conclusion of the Tenth Plenum, Mao scored a partial victory. Although Liu Shao-ch'i, who had originally signed the decree[51] dismissing P'eng Teh-huai in 1959, joined Teng Hsiao-p'ing in proposing that the verdict now be reversed, P'eng Teh-huai was not forgiven. When told of this, P'eng cried, "I'll not keep my mouth shut any more. I want to be a Hai Jui"[52]—a reference to the honest, conscientious Ming official who was dismissed by Emperor Chia Ching for having demanded that the emperor return to the peasants their illegally confiscated land. The plenum, however, shied away from concrete decisions while agreeing on the necessity of reestablishing control over the rural population, which had been severely shaken during years of prolonged crisis. Disorder resulting from the gradual dismantling of the people's communes, lack of food, and difficulties in supply had led not only to general discontent, direct opposition, and acts of resistance in the villages, but also to a slackening of the enthusiasm of basic-level cadres.[53] As an urgent, remedial measure, the Party launched the Socialist Education Movement.

Thus, on May 20, 1963, the Party adopted a "Draft Resolution of the Central Committee of the Chinese Communist Party on Some Problems in Current Rural Work," the blueprint for the Socialist Education Movement.[54] This resolution, reportedly authored by Mao himself and often referred to in its abbreviated form as "The First Ten Points," reflected in essence Mao's views on what should be done in the countryside. Mao repeated his earlier cautions, given at the Peitaiho Conference (1958) and again at the Tenth Plenum (1962), that:

> Socialist society is a relatively long stage; that in this stage there still exist class, class contradiction, and class struggle; and that also existent is the struggle between socialism and capitalism and the danger of a comeback of capitalism.[55]

At first, emphasis was placed on limiting private production by peasants and checking the influence of the old village elites, which had been steadily growing since the 1960s, by reinforcing social classifications implemented during the earlier land reform movement of 1950–53.[56] The importance of poor and lower middle peasants was underscored:

> In rural areas, the proletarian dictatorship can be realized only by relying upon the poor peasants and the lower middle peasants. They are the only ones to rely upon for the formation of a strong alliance of workers and peasants, for the expert management of the nation, for achieving a good collective economy, for the effective suppression and remoulding of all the hostile elements, and for smashing the encirclement formed by the spontaneous capitalist forces.[57]

Furthermore, reliance on these groups should not be a temporary expedient but rather the "long-range class-line of the Party."[58]

The resolution argued for the universal implementation of the Socialist Education Movement in the countryside "in order to demarcate the contradictions between ourselves and the enemy, and the internal contradictions of the people."[59] Finally, citing the rising level of agricultural production, "The First Ten Points" admonished the Liuists by claiming:

> It was groundless for some comrades to entertain pessimistic views in the past towards the rural situation and the conditions of agricultural production.[60]

Meanwhile, in the face of mounting rural resistance to the Socialist Education Movement, the CC issued in September 1963 another directive, "Some

Concrete Policy Formulations of the CC of the CCP in the Rural Socialist Education Movement"—commonly referred to as "The Later Ten Points," and reportedly written under the guidance of P'eng Chen*—modifying "The First Ten Points" in many significant ways. While not denying the importance of the poor and lower middle peasants, it came to the defense of upper middle peasants, claiming:

> They are laborers, and our friends. Therefore, we must endeavor to consolidate them, and enable them to correctly function in production. Since the collectivization more than a decade ago, facts have proved that the great majority of upper-middle peasants are capable of following us on the road to socialism.[61]

"The Later Ten Points" went on to refute Mao's view that the conflicts between the poor and lower middle peasants and the upper middle peasants were the "contradictions between ourselves and the enemy." These were rather internal conflicts of the people, and thus to be "handled with care":[62]

> In opposing a few upper-middle peasants for their tendency toward capitalism, we should only adopt the methods of criticism and education, and should not use the measure of struggle which we adopt against our enemy. We should not deprive them of their rights as commune members, brand those under criticism as capitalists, and, especially, encroach upon their legal profits which they earn by joining in collective labor and earn by laboring more than others. In a few places, some incidents happened in which some upper-middle peasants were subjected to struggle in the same way as landlords during the former land reform. Such incidents should be firmly prevented. To push upper-middle peasants to the side of landlords and rich peasants will be most disadvantageous to us.[63]

The resolution also raised the point that "some poor peasants and other middle peasants are mistakenly classified as upper-middle peasants,"[64] including those "whose living standard has been elevated since the collectivization," as well as those "who have enriched themselves with illegal income after the collectivization."[65] Equally wrong was the use of a "living standard" or "political attitude" as a yardstick for determining the status of peasants; rather, the correct standard should be the "possession of comparatively more production facilities and commitment of only minor exploitations."[66]

Concerned that the earlier progress exemplified by the "Sixty Articles"

---

*Teng Hsiao–p'ing also could have been its author.

would be jeopardized, P'eng Chen demanded, "the Sixty Articles should be strictly followed, and no violation [is] tolerated":

> All problems related to the Sixty Articles should be handled strictly in accordance with the stipulations of the Sixty Articles. The Sixty Articles should in no case be put aside and new methods adopted.[67]

The implication was clear—the success or failure of the Socialist Education Movement would be measured by whether or not the "Sixty Articles" had been "well implemented."[68]

To carry out the objectives of the Socialist Education Movement, the CC sent "work teams" to the countryside. In November 1963, Wang Kuang-mei, the wife of Liu Shao-ch'i, went under an alias to conduct an on-the-spot inspection at a commune in Hopei province. It took her six months to complete her mission and submit a report, entitled "The Experience of the Peach Garden"; Liu deemed the report as having "universal" value and, in the name of the CC, ordered Party organizations at the lower levels to study it.

Ordered by Mao, Liu had to revise "The Later Ten Points" in September 1964. Major features of the earlier document were retained, and all changes were relatively minor. Thus the "Revised Later Ten Points" predicted that the Socialist Education Movement would take some time, "probably five to six years, or even longer,"[69] to accomplish its goals. It proposed the creation of a "class file" of peasants, with the provision that:

> Any mistake in former classification should be duly corrected. In certain districts where the democratic revolution has not been thoroughly carried out, or in districts where no previous class classification has ever been made, a new classification program should be carried out.[70]

Liu's document assumed a more lenient attitude toward cadres as well as those peasants who were the targets of the Socialist Education Movement. The number of cadres who should be punished or expelled from the Party in a *hsien* had been previously set at "within two percent";[71] now it was placed at "around one percent and below two percent."[72] Furthermore, "the great majority of basic-level rural cadres," the document maintained, "are good, or at least are basically good and can stand firm on the road of socialism under the Party's leadership."[73]

Aware of Liu's circumvention of his policies, Mao called for a central work conference in January 1965, and accused Liu of pursuing policies that were "left in form but right in substance" and "not Marxist-Leninist."[74] The conference adopted the "Twenty-three Articles," bearing Mao's personal imprint as it made references to those with "bound feet," urged all communes to "learn from the PLA," and concluded with his favorite topics—"dialectical materialism" and "metaphysics and scholasticism."[75] But apparently Mao faced overwhelming opposition at the conference and was unable to impose his views on the participants, since the "Twenty-three Articles" differed little in substance from the "Revised Later Ten Points," although it was supposed to be "uniformly taken as the standard"[76] in case of conflict with earlier directives. Nevertheless, Mao did not suffer total defeat, for there was in the new document one section that would not please the Liu faction:

> The key point of this movement is to rectify those people in positions of authority within the Party who take the capitalist road, and to progressively consolidate and develop the socialist battlefront in the urban and rural areas.
>
> Of those people in positions of authority who take the capitalist road, some are out in the open and some are concealed. Of the people who support them some are at lower levels and some are at higher levels. Among those lower down, some have already been classified as landlords, rich peasants, counter-revolutionaries and bad elements, while others have been overlooked.
>
> Among those at higher levels, there are some people in the communes, districts, *hsien,* special districts, and even in the work of provincial and Central Committee departments, who oppose socialism. Among them some were originally alien class elements; some are degenerate elements who have shed their original skin and changed their nature; and some have received bribes, banded together for seditious purposes, violated the law, and violated discipline.
>
> Certain people do not distinguish the boundary between the enemy and ourselves; they have lost their class standpoint; and they harbor, within their own families and among their own friends and fellow workers, those people who engage in capitalist activities.
>
> The great majority of our cadres want to take the socialist road, but there are some among them who have but a hazy knowledge of the socialist revolution, who employ personnel improperly, who are haphazard about checking up on work, and who commit the mistake of bureaucratism.[77]

Yet Mao was not satisfied. At a session of the Standing Committee of the Politburo during September–October 1965, with "leading comrades of all the regional bureaus"[78] in attendance, he launched an attack against the rightists by accusing Wu Han, the author of a drama entitled "Hai Jui Dismissed from Office," of using historical allusion to criticize him. Wu had hinted in the play that Mao, like the sixteenth century emperor Chia Ching, had without justification dismissed a good and upright official. A respected figure in literary circles and high official in the Peking MPC, Wu was a close friend of P'eng Chen. The Liuists, as later reports revealed, refused to acquiesce to Mao's wish that they repudiate Wu Han, and in fact, "used every means to counter it."[79] P'eng Chen went as far as to proclaim that "in truth, everyone is equal" and thus, Mao, when wrong, should also be criticized.[80]

## NOTES

1. *(Jen-min Jih-pao), People's Daily,* August 15, 1967.

2. Stuart R. Schram, "Mao Tse-tung and Liu Shao-ch'i, 1939–1969," *Asian Survey, 12* April 1972, p. 276.

3. Ibid., p. 277.

4. Stuart R. Schram et al., *Marxism and Asia* (New York: Penguin Press, 1969), pp. 259–61.

5. Teng Hsiao-p'ing, "Report on the Revision of the Party Constitution to the Eighth Party Congress," *People's Daily,* September 18, 1956.

6. Ibid.

7. Schram, "Mao Tse-tung and Liu Shao-ch'i, 1939–1969," op. cit., p. 279.

8. *China News Analysis,* no. 757 (May 16, 1969), p. 2.

9. See the "General Program" of the "Constitution of the Communist Party of China, 1945," in Peter H. Tang, *Communist China Today (Vol. II): Chronological and Documentary Supplement* (New York: Frederick A. Praeger, 1958), p. 70.

10. Teng Hsiao-p'ing, op. cit.

11. *Kuan-yu Liu Shao-ch'i tang-an ts'ai-liao hui-pien-chi,* Tientsin, Wu-sh'an-chieh-chi chuan-cheng ko-ming tsao-fa ta-tui (April 1967), p. 15, cited by Schram, "Mao Tse-tung and Liu Shao-ch'i, 1939–1969," op. cit., p. 283.

12. "The Struggle between Two Roads in the Chinese Village," *People's Daily,* November 22, 1967.

13. Ibid.

14. A. Doak Barnett, *Uncertain Passage: China's Transition to the Post-Mao Era* (Washington, D.C.: Brookings Institution, 1974), p. 124.

15. Critic, Hung-ch'i *(Red Flag),* no. 12 (1958), quoted by Tsai Hsiao-chien, "Struggle between Mao Tse-tung and Liu Shao-ch'i on the 'Two Different Roads' (3)," *Chung-kung yen-chiu 2 (Studies on Chinese Communism),* no. 3 (March 1968), p. 51.

16. Ibid.

17. *People's Daily,* August 29, 1959, quoted by Tsai Hsiao-chien, "Struggle between Mao Tse-tung and Liu Shao-ch'i on the 'Two Different Roads' (4)," *Studies on Chinese Communism 2,* no. 4 (April 1968), p. 49.

18. "Resolution on Some Questions Concerning the People's Communes" (Wuhan Resolution), *Sixth Plenary Session of the Eighth Central Committee of the Communist Party of China* (Peking: Foreign Languages Press, 1958) pp. 12–49, cited in *Communist China 1955–1959* (Cambridge, Mass.: Harvard University Press, 1962), p. 492.

19. "Decision Approving Comrade's Mao Tse-tung's Proposal That He Will Not Stand as Candidate for Chairman of the People's Republic of China for the Next Term of Office," op. cit., pp. 50–51, cited in *Communist China 1955–1959,* op. cit., p. 487.

20. "Long Live Mao Tse-tung's Thoughts," *People's Daily,* July 1, 1966.

21. "The Wicked History of P'eng Te-huai," *Current Background,* no. 851 (April 26, 1968), p. 19.

22. Ibid., p. 20.

23. Ibid., p. 21.

24. Ibid., p. 24.

25. Ibid., p. 22.

26. Ibid.

27. The acrimonious nature of the dispute, however, was apparent, as Mao claimed that P'eng said at this conference, "You fucked my mother for 40 days, why cannot I fuck your mother for 20 days." *Mao Tse-tung ssu-hsiang wan-sui (Long Live Mao Tse-tung's Thoughts),* (n.p., August 1969), p. 435. For the English translation, see *Current Background,* no. 851 (April 26, 1968), p. 14.

28. *Current Background,* no. 851 (April 26, 1968), p. 14.

29. Union Research Institute, *The Case of P'eng Teh-huai 1959–1968* (Hong Kong: Union Research Institute, 1968) (hereafter, *The Case of P'eng Teh-huai*), p. 14.

30. *Current Background,* no. 851, p. 19.

31. *The Case of P'eng Teh-huai,* p. 14.

32. "Mao Tse-tung's Speech at the Eighth Plenary Session of the CCP Eighth Central Committee," cited in *The Case of P'eng Teh-huai,* p. 21.

33. David A. Charles, "The Dismissal of Marshall P'eng Teh-huai," *The China Quarterly,* no. 8 (October/December 1961), p. 68.

34. For details, see ibid., p. 73, especially footnote 11.

35. "Resolution on Developing the Campaign for Increasing Production and Practicing Economy," *Eighth Plenary Session of the Eighth Central Committee of the Communist Party of China,* op. cit., pp. 8–19, in *Communist China 1955–1959,* op. cit., p. 537.

36. "Resolution on Some Questions Concerning the People's Communes" (Wuhan Resolution), op. cit., *in Communist China 1955–1959,* p. 495; see also *Studies on Chinese Communism 2,* no. 4 (April 1968), p. 52.

37. *Current Background,* no. 652 (April 28, 1969), p. 25.

38. "Big Exposure of a Conspiracy to Usurp the Party and State Leadership," *Survey of China Mainland Press,* no. 4014 (September 5, 1967), p. 2.

39. Ibid., p. 5.

40. Ibid., p. 4.

41. Ibid., p. 6.

42. Ibid., p. 3.

43. Ibid.

44. "Thoroughly Disclosing the Inside Story of 'Ch'ang Kuan Lou' Counter-Revolutionary Incident," *Survey of China Mainland Press,* no. 4001 (August 15, 1967), p. 8.

45. Ibid., p. 4.

46. *Survey of China Mainland Magazines,* no. 651 (April 22, 1969), p. 21, and no. 652 (April 28, 1969), p. 5.

47. *New China News Agency,* August 14, 1967.

48. *Peking Review,* no. 39 (September 28, 1962), p. 7.

49. *Current Background,* no. 851 (April 26, 1968), p. 15.

50. *The Case of P'eng Teh-huai,* p. v.

51. Ibid., p. viii.

52. *Current Background,* no. 851 (April 26, 1968), p. 15.

53. Richard Baum, *Prelude to Revolution: Mao, the Party and the Peasant Question 1962–66* (New York: Columbia University Press, 1975), p. 14.

54. Richard Baum and Frederick Teiwes, *Ssu-ch'ing: The Socialist Education Movement of 1962–1966* (Berkeley: University of California Press, 1968), p. 14.

55. Ibid., p. 60.

56. Jurgen Domes, *The Internal Politics of China 1949–1972* (New York: Praeger, 1973), p. 137.

57. Baum and Teiwes, *Ssu-ch'ing,* op. cit., p. 62.

58. Ibid.

59. Ibid.

60. Ibid., p. 60.

61. Ibid., p. 84.

62. Ibid.

63. Ibid.

64. Ibid., pp. 82–83.

65. I am indebted to Richard Baum for a Chinese text of this document.

66. Baum and Teiwes, *Ssu-ch'ing,* op. cit., p. 83.

67. Ibid.

68. Ibid.

69. Ibid., p. 104.

70. Ibid., p. 110.

71. Ibid., p. 84.

72. Ibid., p. 114.

73. Ibid., p. 112.

74. Philip Bridgham, "Factionalism in the Central Committee," in *Party Leadership and Revolutionary Power,* ed. John Wilson Lewis (London: Cambridge University Press, 1970), p. 229.

75. Baum and Teiwes, *Ssu-ch'ing,* op. cit., p. 126.

76. Ibid., p. 118.

77. Ibid., p. 120.

78. Union Research Institute, *CCP Documents of the Great Proletarian Cultural Revolution* (Hong Kong: Union Research Institute, 1968), p. 20.

79. *Red Flag,* no. 9 (1967).

80. *Joint Publications Research Service,* no. 42349 (August 25, 1967), p. 3.

# 2

## THE CULTURAL REVOLUTION
## AND THE LEFTISTS

Increasingly frustrated by the Party apparatus in Peking, which was so tightly controlled by P'eng Chen that, Mao asserted, it was impossible to "pour in water or stick in a needle,"[1] Mao left in late November 1965 for Shanghai, where he joined his wife, Chiang Ch'ing, and other radical leaders active under the leadership of Yao Wen-yuan and Chang Ch'un-ch'iao. Yao, a minor writer and propagandist, had previously published an article in the November 10, 1965, issue of *Wen Hui Pao* entitled "On the New Historical Play 'Hai Jui Dismissed from Office,' " which attacked the play, written by Wu Han in 1961, as being critical of Mao. Yao's article, written under the supervision of Chiang Ch'ing and personally revised three times by Mao, became the first shot fired by Maoists at their opposition in the initial stages of the Great Proletarian Cultural Revolution.[2]

The article elicited an immediate response from the Liuists. Realizing that as Wu's superior in the Peking MPC, he was most probably Yao's real target, P'eng Chen telephoned the Shanghai MPC and inquired:

What is the background, if any, for you to publish Yao Wen-yuan's article? Why have you not informed us in advance? Where is your party spirit?[3]

To defend Wu, its vice-mayor, the Peking MPC denied through its newspaper that Wu had any malicious intent in writing the play and tried to downgrade his drama to something of mere "academic concern," without political significance. P'eng personally went to Wu's defense and insisted on the latter's innocence.

While Mao sojourned in Shanghai, Liu assumed the chairmanship of the Standing Committee of the Politburo, thus gaining almost complete control over the Party apparatus at the highest level. In February 1966, Liu appointed

P'eng Chen to chair the newly created Cultural Revolution Group or Group of Five, a body charged with the formulation and implementation of policies designed to cleanse intellectual circles of "bourgeois elements" such as Wu Han. Of the other four members of the Cultural Revolution Group, three were members of P'eng's clique: Lu Ting-yi, head of the Propaganda Department of the CC; Chou Yang, minister of culture in the State Council; and Wu Leng-hsi, director of the New China News Agency. Only K'ang Sheng, the semi-invalid chief of intelligence and security, was close to Mao.

The Cultural Revolution Group submitted the results of its investigation of "bourgeois elements" in the "February Report," which, not surprisingly, reached the conclusion that the "Dismissal of Hai Jui" was a purely "academic question" and "contradiction among the people,"[4] and that Wu Han had neither a close personal relationship nor organizational links with P'eng Teh-huai.[5] The report concluded with the subtle allusion:

> One should not be arbitrary like a scholar-tyrant or overwhelm others by the use of one's position or power.[6]

At a special session of the Standing Committee of the Politburo which he convened in Hangchow from March 17 to 20, 1966, Mao was able to engineer the passage of a motion officially condemning P'eng's "February Report":

> It runs counter to the line of the socialist cultural revolution set forth by the Central Committee and Comrade Mao Tse-tung and to the guiding principles formulated at the Tenth Plenary Session of the Eighth Central Committee of the Party in 1962 on the question of classes and class struggle in socialist society. While feigning compliance, the outline actually opposes and stubbornly resists the great cultural revolution initiated and led personally by Comrade Mao Tse-tung.[7]

In the absence of Liu Shao-ch'i, who had left in April for several state visits in Southeast Asia, Chou En-lai, premier of the State Council and third-ranking member of the CCP, took charge of the Secretariat at the special session and decided to support Mao's purge of P'eng Chen. And Teng Hsiao-p'ing, who presided over the session, was persuaded to give in to the purge.[8] Consequently, P'eng's Group of Five was replaced on April 16 with a new organization "directly under the Standing Committee of the Political Bureau [Politburo]"[9]—the Central Cultural Revolution Group (CCRG). Cutting short his visit abroad, Liu hurried back on around April 20, only to discover that it was too late, and without the votes of Chou and Teng, he was clearly in the minority in the seven-man Standing Committee of the Politburo.

On May 16 an enlarged conference of the Politburo adopted a circular that had been "formulated under the personal guidance" of Mao and that officially sealed P'eng Chen's fate:

> The outline report by the so-called 'Group of Five' is actually an outline report by P'eng Chen alone. He concocted it behind the backs of Comrade K'ang Sheng, a member of the 'Group of Five,' and other comrades. P'eng Chen had no discussions or exchange of views at all within the 'Group of Five.' He did not . . . make it clear that it was being sent to the Central Committee for examination as its official document, and still less did he get the approval of Comrade Mao Tse-tung. . . . Employing the most improper methods, he acted arbitrarily, abused his powers and, usurping the name of the Central Committee, hurriedly issued the outline report to the whole Party.[10]

Two days afterward, Lin Piao disclosed the results of his investigation that supposedly exposed the conspiratorial activities of Lu Ting-yi, and of Yang Shang-k'un, director of the General Office of the CC, who had once served as P'eng Teh-huai's political commissar and worked under P'eng Chen and Liu Shao-ch'i in the North China Bureau of the Party. Accused of being the fellow conspirators of P'eng Chen and Lo Jui-ch'ing, Lu Ting-yi and Yang Shang-k'un were charged later, together with Chou Yang, with "anti-Party activities":

> They reached out to grab power in the Party, army, and government. Their aim was to usurp the leadership of the Party, army, and government and to restore capitalism.[11]

P'eng Chen's dismissal was made official on June 3, 1966, when the earlier May 25 reorganization of the Peking MPC was confirmed by the announcement that Li Hsueh-feng, first secretary of the North China Bureau, had been appointed first secretary of the Peking MPC, one of P'eng's posts. As a result of this reorganization, Teng T'o, Liao Mo-sha, and Wu Han were all purged.

The pace of the impending conflict between Mao and Liu accelerated, moving on a collision course. The Liuists feverishly made plans to call a plenum of the CC in July so that the provision for Mao's retirement in the 1956 Party Constitution could be carried out as part of a concerted effort to curtail Mao's authority and influence. Those supporting Mao mounted an offensive of their own; troops commanded by Yang Ch'eng-wu, a supporter of Lin Piao, moved into the capital from nearby Tientsin and occupied Party headquarters.

Yang was appointed acting chief of staff on August 1, 1966, replacing Lo Jui-ch'ing, who had disappeared in November 1965.[12] Lo's dismissal had been long expected, for it had been common knowledge that he had been at odds with Mao over whether political indoctrination or military training should take precedence in the army. Mao believed in "people's wars" and the superiority of ideology over weapons, even nuclear ones; Lo, alarmed by the American entry into the Vietnam struggle in 1965, argued that the PLA should be "professionalized" and "technically improved." Probably more damaging, however, were Lo's intimate relationships with those who opposed Mao. "His cardinal crime," Yang Ch'eng-wu pointed out, "is that over a long period he took his orders from China's Khrushchev."[13] His audacity in supporting Liu went to the extent of "using the term 'two chairmen' and of cheering 'Long Life to Liu' at a New Year's state gathering. His attempts to put Liu on a par with Mao were seen as blasphemy."[14] Lin Piao had personally attacked Lo in a CC work çonference in March 1966 for attempting to "grasp the leadership of the Party, army and government"[15] in collusion with Liu Shao-ch'i, Teng Hsiao-p'ing, and P'eng Chen (who had come to Lo's defense but failed), and for associating with "important members of the counter-revolutionary, anti-Party, anti-socialist clique" in the PLA.[16] Lo tried to kill himself on March 18, 1966, by leaping from the window of a tall building but only succeeded in breaking his leg.

Meanwhile, as Lin Piao's forces gained control of Peking, Mao had ended his eight-month absence and returned on July 18, 1966. The meeting at which Liu had hoped to unseat Mao never materialized, and in its place, the Eleventh Plenum of the Eighth CC, called by Mao, met on August 1, 1966.

## THE ELEVENTH PLENUM AND THE FALL OF LIU SHAO-CH'I

This plenum, the first since 1962, despite the Party Constitution stipulation that one be held "every two years," was obviously a Maoist-stacked gathering. The names of the regular and alternate members of the CC who attended the meeting were never made public. Only 46 regular members and 33 alternates out of a total membership of 181, or about 46 percent, actually participated.[17] The participation of constitutionally unauthorized groups, such as the "representatives of the revolutionary teachers and students," was openly acknowledged.[18] Yet Mao barely managed to get his program passed, admitting: "Many people could not be converted to my view."[19]

Lin Piao, unveiled for the first time as Mao's most trusted supporter, delivered the keynote address at the plenum in which he unequivocally stated that loyalty to Mao and his ideology was the only means of determining a good Communist:

> ... I will rely on the Chairman.
> ... Chairman Mao is the axle; we are the wheel. We must do everything according to Mao Tse-tung thought and not by any other method. We should not be two headquarters opposing each other. We should be united following the Chairman ...

I have no talent; I rely on the wisdom of the masses and do everything according to the Chairman's directives. The Chairman is the genius of the world revolution.[20]

Ignoring the Party Constitution, which permitted changes in leadership only at Party Congresses, Mao used the plenum to reshuffle the Party's top leadership; Liu Shao-ch'i fell to eighth position and was thereby excluded from the seven-member Standing Committee, while Lin Piao rose to second position and was named sole vice-chairman. Chou En-lai remained third but no longer held the position of vice-chairman. Surprisingly, T'ao Chu, first secretary of the CCP's South China Bureau, rose to fourth position and upon recommendation of Teng Hsiao-p'ing, became the new chief of the Propaganda Department. Ranked below T'ao were Ch'en Po-ta, Teng Hsiao-p'ing, and K'ang Sheng, in that order.[21] Two other vice-chairmen, Chu Teh and Ch'en Yün, were demoted and ranked below Liu Shao-ch'i. Chu Teh and Ch'en Yün had voted against Mao at a Standing Committee meeting called to strip Liu of his authority, although both had been in disfavor far longer. Chu Teh, Mao's Long March comrade and former commander in chief, had disagreed with the Chairman in the past.[22] Ch'en Yün, an economist, had opposed Mao's Great Leap program.

## The "Sixteen Points"

The plenum issued the "Sixteen Points" as a guideline for conducting the Great Proletarian Cultural Revolution, a "great revolution that touches people to their very souls":

At present, our objective is to struggle against and crush those persons in authority who are taking the capitalist road, to criticize and repudiate the reactionary bourgeois academic 'authorities' and the ideology of the bourgeoisie and all other exploiting classes and to transform education, literature and art and all other parts of the superstructure that do not correspond to the socialist economic base, so as to facilitate the consolidation and development of the socialist system.[23]

Vividly, the "Sixteen Points" described the ways in which those "taking the capitalist road" had operated in the past:

Some units are controlled by those who have wormed their way into the Party and are taking the capitalist road. Such persons in authority are extremely afraid of being exposed by the masses and therefore seek every possible pretext to suppress the mass movement. They resort to such tactics as shifting the targets for attack and turning black into white in an attempt to lead the movement astray. When they find themselves very isolated and no longer able to carry on as before, they resort still more to intrigues, stabbing people in the back, spreading rumors, and blurring the distinction between revolution and counter-revolution as much as they can, all for the purpose of attacking the revolutionaries.[24]

Yet the "Sixteen Points" showed distinct signs of being a compromise document bearing the imprint of many hands. Chou probably extracted from the Maoists the concession that many sectors of China would be sheltered from the coming political storm. Industrial and agricultural production, for example, according to the "Sixteen Points" were not to be hindered by the activities of the Cultural Revolution, and the nuclear weapons technicians were to be exempted as long as they "love their country, work actively, and not against the Party and socialism, and do not secretly collaborate with any foreign power." The army demanded and received permission to conduct its own "socialist education movement" without any external interference, circumventing both the student activists and the CCRG in the Party.

Other members of the Party hierarchy not aligned with Liu were able to press for the adoption of self-protecting devices. Distinctions were drawn between "good" Party members who "encourage the masses," and bad elements who "do their best to confuse the boundary line between revolution and counter-revolution." The majority of Party cadres were characterized as "good," and those beyond redemption as only a "small number." The "Sixteen Points" even had a provision that no campaigns of criticism should be undertaken against supposed "reactionaries" without prior discussion and approval by Party committees "at the corresponding levels." As shown later, Party cadres under attack were to cite these statements in their own defense.

Those supporting Mao were probably responsible for the reiteration of the "mass line," urging everyone to "trust the masses, rely on them and respect their initiative," and most likely introduced the following into the "Sixteen Points":

Cast out fear. Don't be afraid of disorder. Chairman Mao has often told us that revolution cannot be so very refined, so gentle, so temperate, kind, courteous, restrained and magnanimous.[25]

Such belligerent exhortations might have given rebellious students a rationale to use force even though they were later told officially to rely on persuasion rather than intimidation. Any youth looking for an excuse for violence could find it in Mao's own saying, "No construction without destruction."[26]

## THE RISE OF LIN PIAO

In 1959, when Lin Piao replaced P'eng Teh-huai as minister of defense, the morale and combat effectiveness of the PLA had declined as a result of the collapse of the Great Leap, the subsequent agricultural depression and withdrawal of Soviet aid, and the Party's deteriorated political apparatus inside the PLA. Yet the gravity of the situation presented Lin with a great professional challenge, as well as an opportunity to increase his influence in the military establishment.

Though he reappointed four of the seven vice-ministers in the Ministry of Defense who had no close relationship with P'eng, Lin also appointed six additional vice-ministers to strengthen his control.[27] Lin, however, cleaned house more thoroughly in PLA headquarters, reducing the original seven departments to three and placing his men in charge wherever possible. Despite the fact that Lo Jui-ch'ing, usually identified with the North China Field Army, became the new chief of staff and took control of the General Staff Department upon the recommendation of Liu Shao-ch'i,[28] Ch'iu Hui-tso, a member of the Fourth Field Army elite whose close relationship with Lin was well known, became the director of the Rear Services Department; and Lo Jung-huan resumed his position as director of the General Political Department after T'an Cheng, a surviving vice-minister, was dismissed for opposing Lin's policy of emphasizing the study of Mao's thoughts in the army. After his death, Lo Jung-huan was succeeded by Hsiao Hua, who also had served at one time under Lin.

As minister of defense, Lin took charge of the Military Affairs Commission (MAC) after the Eighth Plenum,[29] and the powers deriving from such a position were so extensive that he had a free hand in carrying out what he personally considered to be the most necessary programs. Immediately after he assumed the post, Lin made strenuous and apparently successful efforts to improve the political reliability and morale of the troops. There was a reorganization and expansion of the political apparatus in the PLA, especially at the basic company level, to insure the "absolute control" of the Party over the armed forces under the slogan "politics in command." The superiority of the Party committees at each level was stressed and the authority of the political commissars enhanced.

As soon as he took office, Lin authorized an article pledging "the unconditional loyalty of the PLA" to Mao and eulogizing Mao's thoughts.[30] He was the only contributor among top Party leaders to a publication of Mao's *Selected Works* in 1960.[31] Thus from 1960 on, Lin so closely associated his own views with those of Mao that the views of the two eventually converged,[32] and Lin was honored for having "creatively"[33] applied the thoughts of Mao, as Mao had "creatively applied the teachings of Lenin and Stalin."[34] It may not be an exaggeration to state that Lin's shrewd promotion of Mao's thought was a means to expand his own influence and one of the principle factors in his rise to power. The *Bulletin of Activities of the PLA,* for example, indicates that Lin's name overshadowed that of every other Party leader (with the exception of Mao) in the armed forces by early 1961.[35]

Lin's measures for restoring the strength and reliability of the armed forces were so successful that the CC gave him a commendation in September of 1962, and by late 1963 Mao was sufficiently satisfied with Lin's innovations to consider them worthy of emulation. With the top Party officials increasingly apathetic to his leadership, Mao turned more frequently to Lin and the PLA. In February 1964, Mao was instrumental in launching the "Learn from the PLA"[36] campaign. Not just another ideological exercise, this nationwide campaign directed all industrial, commercial, and financial ministries, and their subordinate offices, to establish military-style political departments, and to emulate the PLA political commissar system.[37] Lin was thus given the opportunity to infiltrate all levels of the Party and the economy with carefully indoctrinated and personally loyal military men. Some PLA political commissars were commissioned to carry out "continuous investigation" of Party cadres in cultural and ideological work.[38] Even though these commissars' first loyalties were supposedly to the Party, their introduction into the Party's own structure represented the penetration of one Party faction by another, for in many cases the PLA-run political departments duplicated those created by the Party.

The extent of penetration by Lin's "party-soldiers"[39] into the upper echelons of the government can be gauged by the revelation in 1965 that some 200,000 alone were working in offices concerned with trade and finance. Concurrently expanding the armament industry, Lin created three new Ministries of Machine Building in 1963 and an additional two in 1965. Chosen as ministers of these governmental industries were three generals, one admiral, and only one civilian.[40] Even a general and a political commissar were appointed as Vice-Ministers of culture in 1965.[41] It is true that in the military organizations below the national level, few changes took place in the Military Regions (MR) after Lin became the minister of defense; only 5 of 13 commanders and 5 to 7 political commissars were replaced. However, this was not the case in the Military Districts (MD). A large majority of the commanders and political commissars in the MDs directly or indirectly owed their appointments to Lin, and staffs of the PLA and Party hierarchy became more closely intertwined. By 1965, MR commanders were given concurrent posts as secretaries in all but one of the regional bureaus of the Party, and about half the political commissars in the MDs were appointed secretaries in their respective PPCs.[42] Furthermore, Lin had by then gained a firm control over the public security forces when Lo Jui-ch'ing, the minister of public security, came under fire.

Indicative of Lin's continued rise in stature and influence was the important document, "Long Live the Victory of the People's War,"[43] which he authored in September of 1965, an honor reserved usually for Mao himself or Liu Shao-ch'i. This article was given extensive publicity in China and abroad and was one of the documents mentioned in the communique of the Eleventh Plenum. During 1965 Lin intensified the propagation of Mao's thought through the *Liberation Army Daily,* and published for general consumption the *Selected Readings of Mao Tse-tung's Writings,* originally circulated among PLA forces on Lin's instructions in 1961.

When Mao named Lin his sole vice-chairman, he therefore rewarded a man who had carefully and methodically extended his influence first over the military establishment and then the nation. Whether Lin had plotted from the beginning to become Mao's eventual heir, as later charged, is open to question, but there is little doubt that he almost single-mindedly made the PLA more responsive to Mao's wishes and, at the same time, himself Mao's most loyal supporter.

## THE SPREAD OF STUDENT DISCONTENT

In the 1960s, discontent and unrest grew among students in China's schools and colleges as the composition of the student body changed. Young people receiving advanced education during the 1950s were frequently the children of upper-level bureaucrats and technocrats whose background had prepared them well for intense academic competition, but by 1965 new social elements had been introduced into the hitherto fairly homogeneous student population as a result of Mao's attempt to bridge the gulf "between the intellectual aristocracy and the illiterate masses,"[44] a condition he deplored on numerous occasions. Mao hoped to resolve this dilemma and achieve his objective of "converting students into proletarians and proletarians into students"[45] by lowering admission standards, providing scholarships for children of proletarian background, and dispatching students to communes and factories to "learn from the masses."

Class differences began to manifest themselves in the classroom as the old conflict of "red versus expert" was expanded to the field of education. Proletarian youngsters found themselves ill-equipped to compete with the better-prepared children of the bourgeoisie who, on the other hand, complained about the dilution of the quality of their education. Furthermore, working-class children were deeply disappointed when they discovered that, contrary to the official propaganda line of the Party, which asserted the leadership role of the proletariat, "the existing system meant their academic and social humiliation at the hands of the middle class whom they have been taught to distrust."[46]

When economic depression followed the Great Leap fiasco, students from all classes suffered. No longer could they hope to utilize the skills gained through their education; instead, all they could expect after graduation was manual labor in the countryside—a dead end, in the opinion of urban and peasant students alike. Frustrated and disillusioned, the students found a ready scapegoat—the Party. As they became openly critical of all authority, they formed loosely knit groups to voice their discontent. In May of 1966, Tsinghua Middle School students were organized[47] and later clashed with the Party work team sent to conduct the Socialist Education Movement and to pacify students who had become increasingly radical in their demands. At first the work team was not confronted with an impossible task since the students organized to resist them were neither extremely militant nor well directed. During June and July of 1966, the work teams met with considerable success and in all probability would have subdued the activists were it not for Mao Tse-tung's intervention.

At Peking University, familiarly known as Peita, a group of radical students led by Nieh Yuan-tzu, an instructor in the philosophy department and a Party secretary, and six other "tough nuts,"[48] were engaged in a feud with Lu P'ing, the president of the university and close friend of P'eng Chen, and the university Party Committee sympathetic to Lu. Lu mobilized members of the Peita Communist Youth League whose rolls contained a disproportionate number of students from "bourgeois" backgrounds, branded Nieh and her supporters "renegades" and "anti-Party elements," and proclaimed that his committee was the genuine "Marxist-Leninist Party Committee" and "to oppose the school's Party organ is to oppose the Party Central Committee and to oppose Lu P'ing is to oppose the Party."[49]

When the contents of the "May 16th Circular" were made known on the Peita campus on May 18, 1966, Nieh and the radical students, realizing that they had been correct in their criticisms all along, put up a big-character poster on May 25 attacking Lu P'ing; Sung Shuo, the representative of the Universities Department of the Peking MPC; and P'eng P'ei-yun, a vice-secretary of the Peita Party Committee:

> You 'lead' the masses not to hold meetings and not to put up big-character posters. You have manufactured various taboos and regulations. By so doing, have you not suppressed the mass revolution, forbidden it, and opposed it? We absolutely won't allow you to do so![50]

## Wide-Scale Fighting and Mao's Intervention

Fighting broke out on a wide scale and the radicals increasingly became the target of attack. In the following week, Mao entered the fracas by telephoning K'ang Sheng from Shanghai on June 1 with the order to publish and broadcast, "at once," "the wall poster written by Nieh Yuan-tzu and six other comrades."[51]

Shortly after midnight on June 2, Wu Teh, second secretary of the Peking MPC, arrived at Peita with news of the purge of P'eng Chen and the dismissal of Lu P'ing and P'eng P'ei-yun "from all their posts."[52] Meanwhile, Liu sent new work teams to the various Peking campuses, and his wife, Wang Kuang-mei, was one of their key members. Little is known about her activities at Peita, but at Tsinghua University, where she also went, on June 21, 1966:

She branded more than 800 revolutionary teachers and students represented by Comrade K'uai Ta-fu 'counter-revolutionaries,' 'pseudo-leftists but genuine rightists,' and spread.white terror that brought about the death of one person and caused many persons to commit suicide.[53]

The tug-of-war between the radicals and the Liu-directed work teams continued until Mao's return to Peking on July 18, when he immediately expressed his disapproval of the work teams' suppression of the dissident students. On July 22, Chiang Ch'ing, Ch'en Po-ta, and K'ang Sheng, all members of the CCRG, visited Peita several times, and on July 26, the Party work team sent there by Liu was disbanded and discredited. In a directive to Lin Piao, Mao declared that "the domination of our schools by bourgeois intellectuals should by no means be allowed to continue."[54] At a meeting on July 29, 1966, Mao, Chou, and other Party leaders blessed a contingent of students from several Peking schools, and the name Red Guards was probably adopted at this meeting.

Having earlier praised Nieh's poster as "China's first Marxist-Leninist big-character poster," Mao composed his own on August 5 called "Bombard the Headquarters," the first and only time he would make such an undisguised reference to his primary target in the Cultural Revolution, the Liuist-dominated Party. Emotionally upbraiding those who opposed his revolution, Mao wrote:

They have enforced a bourgeois dictatorship and struck down the surging movement of the great cultural revolution of the proletariat. They have stood facts on their head and juggled black and white, encircled and suppressed revolutionaries, stifled opinions differing from their own, imposed a White Terror, and felt very pleased with themselves. They have puffed up the arrogance of the bourgeoisie and deflated the morale of the proletariat. How vicious they are![55]

Few knew at the time that Mao had approved the dispatching of work teams to the schools and universities in order to trap Liu Shao-ch'i and his supporters in anticipation of their noncompliance, as he had revealed at a Party meeting in mid-July:

Some comrades are very ferocious when they struggle against other people, but are unable to wage struggle against themselves. They will never be able to pass the test in this way.

When you are told to kindle a fire to burn yourselves, will you do it? After all, you yourselves will be burned.

Be prepared for the revolution coming over your own head. Leaders of the Party and the government and responsible comrades of the Party must be so prepared.[56]

The Red Guards did not receive official national recognition until the famous rally of August 18, 1966. Mao, symbolically dressed in a PLA uniform to signify his close relationship with the army, made a public appearance at the demonstration honoring the one million Red Guards assembled in front of Tien An Men Square. Lin Piao, however, gave the keynote address, excessively praising Mao:

Chairman Mao is the most outstanding leader of the proletariat in the present era and the greatest genius in the present era. ... Mao Tse-tung's thought marks a completely new stage in the development of Marxism-Leninism. It is Marxism-Leninism at the highest level in the present era. It is Marxism-Leninism for remolding the souls of the people. It is the most powerful ideological weapons of the proletariat.[57]

## THE EMERGENCE OF CHIANG CH'ING

On the reviewing stand at Mao's side during the August 18 rally stood his wife, Chiang Ch'ing, who had hitherto remained in the background and abstained from politics. Now for the first time Chiang spoke publicly on political matters, exhorting the Red Guards to "unite with the revolutionary Left and further develop the Red Guard organization."[58] Such a display of active political participation in one of the most dramatic events in Chinese Communist history was unusual for Chiang who, according to a widely circulated rumor, had agreed years ago not to become "politically or publicly active"[59] in exchange for the departure for Moscow of Mao's second wife, Ho Tse-chen, and the continuation of her living arrangements with Mao. Neither as a Shanghai actress in the 1930s nor as an enthusiastic participant in the cultural field later did Chiang have a distinguished career or recognition for artistic ability and talent. In fact, despite her intimate relationship with Mao, she was "totally rejected by the literary and art circles"[60] in Yenan days, and even after the Communist takeover in 1949, was not invited to join the All-China Federation of Literary and Art Circles, formed by the Propaganda Department of the CC, to which almost all workers in the cultural sphere, including those with only a minor reputation, received invitations.

Undeterred, Chiang remained active, devoting herself to the reform of Chinese opera by incorporating Western music and ballet with traditional Chinese stories and revolutionary tales. While the cultural establishment continued to ignore her, she was praised for her "professional" abilities and "high level of accomplishments" by Lin Piao, who was not unaware of the political advantages to be reaped by such gestures. Lin asked her to sponsor a "seminar for cultural workers in the troops" in January 1966, and in November Chiang was appointed the PLA's adviser on cultural matters[61] when many dance and opera troupes were incorporated into the PLA.

When the CCRG made known its membership, Chiang appeared as its first deputy head under Ch'en Po-ta, Mao's personal secretary, ghostwriter on ideological issues, and chief editor of *Red Flag* since 1958. The importance of the CCRG soon became apparent, as Chou En-lai revealed:

> The Central Cultural Revolution Group is the staff headquarters of the Great Proletarian Cultural Revolution. Under the direct leadership of Chairman Mao and Vice-chairman Lin, it is equal to the former Secretariat of the Central Committee, but the responsibilities it shoulders are even greater than those of the latter.[62]

Directly under Ch'en and Chiang were two advisers, T'ao Chu and K'ang Sheng; three deputy heads, Wang Jen-chung, Liu Chih-chien, and Chang Ch'un-ch'iao; and ten regular members: Chang P'ing-hua, Wang Li, Kuan Feng, Ch'i Pen-yu, Mu Hsin, Yao Wen-yuan, Hsieh Ch'ang-hou, Liu Wei-chen, Cheng Chi-ch'iao, and Yang Chih-lin.

These individuals had one thing in common: most of them lacked a power base of their own, and whatever power they did wield came directly from their relationship to Mao and their fidelity to his ideals. In this respect, the CCRG was a modern version of an ancient device used by China's emperors when the rulers felt their subordinates were not trustworthy—the Inner Court[63]—and later became the backbone of the Left faction. A few members came directly from Chiang's clique. Yao Wen-yuan, the ultraleftist writer, and Chang Ch'un-ch'iao, the director of propaganda of the Shanghai MPC, had collaborated with Madame Mao on the article "On the Dismassal of Hai Jui,"[64] and Chang was even more intimately connected with Chiang Ch'ing through his promotion of her new versions of operas and films dedicated to the revolution.[65] Many have suggested that this relationship contributed greatly toward Chang's swift ascendency to national power.[66]

With an organized base and the support of Mao, Chiang rose rapidly in the Party hierarchy. The General Political Department officially announced that, when the Cultural Revolution Group of the PLA was reorganized on January 11, 1967, Chiang Ch'ing was named an adviser to this group. By now, she had become in her own right a contending force in the swift currents of the Cultural Revolution.

## RAMPAGE OF THE RED GUARDS

After the August 18 rally, the Red Guard movement rapidly gained momentum. Tens of thousands of students from all over the country swarmed the nation's capital, and eventually eleven million young people could claim to have gotten a glimpse of Mao. Under Mao's continuing encouragement, the Red Guards grew in number and, only a month after their formation, became increasingly bold and unruly. Not content with mere parades and demonstrations, they turned toward the destruction of remnants of China's ancient culture such as temples and historic sites; arrested without authorization officials and civilians whom they regarded as bourgeois and physically tortured them; and attacked at will any government organization or office which they considered "revisionist." Mao, however, did not seem to be disturbed, for he said in a speech to a CC work conference in August 1966:

> I firmly believe that a few months of disturbances will be mostly for the good, and that little bad will result from these disturbances. It does not matter if there are no provincial Party committees; we still have the district and *hsien* committees. . . . Workers, peasants and soldiers must not interfere with the students in the great Cultural Revolution.[67]

And *People's Daily* quoted Mao as saying, "In the best analysis, all the truths of Marxism-Leninism can be summed up in one sentence: 'To rebel is justified.' "[68]

The Red Guards' disruptive behavior prompted the Party to take some restrictive action: On September 8, 1966, the CC and the State Council decreed that the Red Guards "should cooperate with the Party and government organizations and with the PLA in shouldering the glorious responsibility of protecting the Party and State secrets," including "codes, telegrams, secret documents, files and secret materials";[69] and prohibited them from touching "the codes, files and secret materials of the Party and government organizations" or forcing their way into offices or archives where such information is stored.[70] On September 14, 1966, the CC, concerned with the autumn harvest, forbade Red Guards to interfere with the functions of Party and government organizations in "communes and brigades below the county level" or "to participate in debates at the various levels below the county."[71] On the surface, the Red Guards seemed to be acting independently, but in reality the military forces loyal to Lin Piao, while officially maintaining a neutral position, gave them moral and material support. Six thousand army vehicles, for example, were allocated for Red Guard use in Peking alone.[72] The PLA served as the model for the Red Guards, and the Red Guards were referred to as "revolutionary small generals" and the "reserves" of the PLA. Sympathetic soldiers provided them with food, shelter, transportation, and guidance, since, reportedly, a "PLA delegate" accompanied every 20 or 30 Red Guards on their excursions around the countryside "to exchange revolutionary experiences."[73] In fact, hundreds of thousands of soldiers were involved in one way or another.[74]

In the provinces as in Peking, Party organizations were the Red Guards' primary targets. Finding themselves under attack, Party cadres devised ingenious ways of defending themselves. Usually, they suppressed or "misinterpreted" central directives with which they did not agree; sacrificed minor or disliked officials to simulate compliance; or, finally, created their own Red Guard bands to compete with the Peking-backed groups or other hostile elements. In some cases, the Party mobilized workers, peasants, and some local military who resented the turmoil created by outside intruders to combat the radicals. Peking was well aware of these diceptions and circumventions. *People's Daily,* for example, reported that "responsible persons in some localities and units" had "openly defied" the 16-point directive and had "created various pretexts to suppress the mass movement . . . and even provoked a number of workers and peasants . . . to oppose and antagonize the revolutionary students."[75]

As the Cultural Revolution spread, the Red Guard groups proliferated. Some groups had thousands of members, others only a few. A youth could belong to several groups at the same time, switching his allegiance from one to another as his fancy dictated. Lacking internal discipline from the very beginning, the groups were prone to argue and fight among themselves. Thus, violence and bloodshed became a normal part of the Red Guard movement. The economy began to show signs of great strain. China's fragile rail system, barely adequate to meet transportation needs under the best of circumstances, broke down as millions of Red Guards traveled free "to make revolution." Industrial production fell when workers deserted factories to fight against the Red Guards; and in many areas, peasants, preoccupied with resisting the disorderly Red Guards, were forced to neglect their farm work, directly undermining agricultural production.

## CHOU EN-LAI AS A MODERATING INFLUENCE

Among the top leadership in Peking, only Chou En-lai seemed concerned about the ominous signals of impending catastrophe. Not so enthusiastic a proponent of the Cultural Revolution as the Maoists, Chou, the chief administrator of China, was in a unique position to appreciate the difficulties resulting from such nationwide disruption. A practical, pragmatic bureaucrat, he repeatedly counseled moderation:

Industry and agriculture cannot take a vacation in order to stage revolution.
. . . Production and the service trades cannot be suspended. Otherwise, what
shall we eat?[76]

Giving the appearance of praising the goals of the Cultural Revolution but
at the same time attempting to insulate sectors of Chinese society from disruption, Chou said in his speech to the third Red Guard rally on September 15,
1966:

. . . the Great Proletarian Cultural Revolution is aimed at revolutionizing the
ideology of man so that greater, faster, better and more economical results
will be attained in all fields of work.
To expedite the normal progress of industrial and agricultural production,
Red Guards and revolutionary students of universities and middle schools
are not to go to industrial plants and business units, organs and agencies
below the *hsien* level, and rural people's communes to exchange revolutionary experience and establish revolutionary ties.[77]

Chou, concealing his contempt for some Red Guards who, as he put it,
"have acted like hooligans," nevertheless spent many patient hours trying to
persuade them to pursue the goals of the Cultural Revolution more peacefully,
but to no avail. They continued to break into government offices, disrupted
normal operation of factories, and fought among themselves, and the list of
injuries and casualties steadily mounted. Chou himself became the victim of
vicious verbal attacks and was forced to compromise.

That there was sharp disagreement regarding the scope and pace of the
Cultural Revolution among the top leadership gradually became visible. While
Chou, supported by the government bureaucracy and some local military
commanders, emphasized moderation and control, the radicals were more
interested in sustaining the revolutionary momentum. Conflicting orders ema-
nating from the CC generated more confusion, and disorder escalated. At
Chiang Ch'ing's urging, about 70 Red Guards on December 4, 1966, "invaded
P'eng Chen's home, climbed over the fence, cut telephone wires and hauled
the former Peking boss trembling out of bed. P'eng was said to have been
brought before a rally of 10,000 Red Guards and denounced to his face on
December 12."[78] Many subordinates of P'eng in the Peking municipal government and its Party committee, such as Liu Jen and Wan I, were also seized.
Apprehended at the same time were other conspicuous members of Liu's
clique such as Lu Ting-yi, Lo Jui-ch'ing, and Yang Shang-kun. Red Guards
from Peking, reportedly, flew to Chengtu in remote Szechwan province to seize
P'eng Teh-huai.[79] All were humiliated and mistreated.

The Maoists even succeeded in reversing the earlier decision to shelter
agriculture from the Cultural Revolution by issuing a 10-point directive on

December 15, 1966, which encouraged Red Guards to go to the countryside to "revolutionize" peasants and "expedite" agricultural production.[80] On December 26, *People's Daily* announced a further expansion of the Cultural Revolution to mines and factories, and the New Year's joint editorial of 1967, by *People's Daily, Liberation Army Daily,* and *Red Flag,* stated that "if the movement stops at the offices, schools, and cultural circles, the Great Proletarian Cultural Revolution would be abolished half-way."[81] The Red Guards now ran rampant everywhere. Provincial party officials found themselves in an "untenable"[82] position, and by early 1967 Party committees at all levels in most cases had "ceased to function."[83] The Peking central authorities, Mao admitted to Edgar Snow in late 1970, had clearly lost control over the Red Guards by the early months of 1967. Since the Maoists had failed to create a new system of effective rule to replace the one being destroyed, China fell into total chaos by January of 1967.

# NOTES

1. Mao Tse-tung, "Speech to the Albanian Military Delegation in Peking" (August 31, 1967), in Institute for the Study of Chinese Communist Problems, *Important CCP Documents of the Great Proletarian Cultural Revolution* (Taipei: Institute for the Study of Chinese Communist Problems, 1973), p. 209; *Survey of China Mainland Press,* no. 4200 (June 18, 1968), pp. 1–5.

2. Stephen Uhalley, Jr., "The Cultural Revolution and the Attack on the 'Three Family Village,' " *The China Quarterly,* no. 27 (July/September 1966), pp. 149–61.

3. *Red Flag,* no. 7 (1966) in *Survey of China Mainland Magazines,* no. 529 (June 20, 1966), p. 2.

4. "Outline Report on the Current Academic Discussion Made by the Group of Five in Charge of the Cultural Revolution" ("February Outline Report"), in Union Research Institute, *CCP Documents on the Great Proletarian Cultural Revolution 1966–1967* (Hong Kong: Union Research Institute, 1968) (hereafter cited as *CCP Documents*), pp. 7–12.

5. *Joint Publications Research Service,* no. 42349 (August 25, 1967), p. 5.

6. *Peking Review,* no. 24 (June 10, 1966), p. 10.

7. "Circular of the Central Committee of the Chinese Communist Party, May 16, 1966," *People's Daily,* May 17, 1967; *Peking Review,* no. 21 (May 19, 1967), pp. 6–9.

8. Edward E. Rice, *Mao's Way* (Berkeley: University of California Press, 1972), p. 239.

9. *People's Daily,* May 17, 1967.

10. *Peking Review,* no. 21 (May 19, 1967), pp. 6–9.

11. *People's Daily,* July 1, 1966.

12. William W. Whitson, *The Chinese High Command: A History of Communist Military Politics, 1927–1971* (New York: Praeger, 1973), p. 370.

13. Lois D. Tretiak, "Revolt of the Generals," *Far Eastern Economic Review 53,* no. 9 (November 30, 1967), p. 409.

14. Ibid.

15. *People's Daily,* July 1, 1966.

16. *Chieh-fang chun-pao (Liberation Army Daily),* August 1, 1966, in *Peking Review,* no. 32 (August 5, 1966), p. 9.

17. *Seikai shuho* (Tokyo), no. 37 (September 13, 1966), quoted in Parris H. Chang, "Provin-

cial Party Leaders' Strategies," in *Elites in the People's Republic of China,* ed. Robert Scalapino (Seattle: University of Washington Press, 1972), p. 36.

18. *People's Daily,* August 14, 1966.

19. "A Talk by Chairman Mao to Foreign Visitors," *Survey of China Mainland Press,* no. 4200 (June 18, 1968), p. 2.

20. *The Lin Piao Affair: Power Politics and Military Coup,* ed. Michael Y. M. Kau (White Plains, N.Y.: International Arts and Sciences Press, 1975), p. 348.

21. *Current Scene 4,* no. 16 (September 5, 1966), p. 2.

22. Chu Teh refused to make a public self-criticism during the Cultural Revolution and intimated that if anyone needed to do so, it was Mao. Rice, op. cit., p. 340.

23. *CCP Documents,* pp. 42–43.

24. Ibid., p. 45.

25. Ibid.

26. *People's Daily,* June 4, 1966; *Peking Review,* no. 24 (June 10, 1966), p. 14.

27. See John Gittings, *The Role of the Chinese Army* (New York: Oxford University Press, 1967), p. 284.

28. Whitson, op. cit., p. 357.

29. Union Research Institute, *The Case of P'eng Teh-huai 1959–1968* (Hong Kong: Union Research Institute, 1968) (hereafter, *The Case of P'eng Teh-huai*), p. 149.

30. Lin Piao, "March Ahead under the Red Flag of the General Line and Mao Tse-tung's Military Thinking," *People's Daily,* September 30, 1959.

31. Lin Piao, "The Victory of the Chinese People's Revolutionary War is the Victory of the Thought of Mao Tse-tung," *Survey of China Mainland Magazines,* no. 231 (October 18, 1960), p. 7.

32. Ralph L. Powell, "The Increasing Power of Lin Piao and the Party-Soldiers 1959–1966," *The China Quarterly,* no. 34 (April/June 1968), p. 50.

33. Institute for the Study of Chinese Communist Problems, *1967 Yearbook on Chinese Communism* (Taipei: Institute for the Study of Chinese Communist Problems, 1967), p. 259.

34. *Current Scene 6,* no. 10 (June 15, 1968), p. 7.

35. "Bulletin of Activities of the PLA," no. 24, in *The Politics of the Chinese Red Army: A Translation of the Bulletin of Activities of the People's Liberation Army,* ed. J. Chester Chen et al. (Stanford: Hoover Institution, 1966), pp. 617–31.

36. See "The Whole Country Must Learn from the PLA," *People's Daily,* February 1, 1964.

37. Philip Bridgham, "Mao's 'Cultural Revolution': Origin and Development," *The China Quarterly,* no. 29 (January/March 1967), p. 11.

38. Ibid.

39. Powell, op. cit., p. 38.

40. Colina MacDougall, "Peking and the PLA," *Far Eastern Economic Review 52,* no. 10 (June 16, 1966), pp. 564–65.

41. See "Hsiao Wang-tung," in Union Research Institute, *Who's Who in Communist China* (Hong Kong: Union Research Institute, 1966), p. 223; cited in Powell, op. cit., p. 48.

42. Rice, op. cit., pp. 201–02.

43. *Peking Review,* no. 36 (September 3, 1965), pp. 9–30.

44. John Israel, "The Red Guards in Historical Perspective," *The China Quarterly,* no. 30 (April/June 1967), pp. 3–4.

45. Ibid.

46. Ibid., p. 4.

47. Ibid., p. 7.

48. These were Sung I-hsiu, Hsia Chien-chia, Yang K'e-ming, Chao Ching-yi, Kao Yun-p'eng and Li Hsing-ch'en, in Victor Nee, *The Cultural Revolution at Peking University* (New York: Monthly Review Press, 1969), p. 54.

49. *New China News Agency,* June 5, 1966; *Peking Review,* no. 24 (June 10, 1966), pp. 14–15.

50. *People's Daily,* June 2, 1966.

51. "Down with Liu Shao-ch'i," *Current Background,* no. 834 (August 17, 1967), p. 26.

52. *New China News Agency,* June 5, 1966; *Peking Review,* no. 24 (June 10, 1966), p. 3.

53. *Current Background,* no. 834 (August 17, 1967), p. 27.

54. *Survey of China Mainland Magazines (Supp.),* no. 18 (February 26, 1968), p. 30, cited in Stanley Karnow, *Mao and China: From Revolution to Revolution* (New York: Viking Press, 1972), p. 170.

55. Mao Tse-tung, "Bombard the Headquarters—My First Big-Character Poster" (August 5, 1966), *Current Background,* no. 891 (October 8, 1969), p. 63.

56. "Mao Tse-tung Talks to Central Committee Leaders," (July 21, 1966), *Current Background,* no. 891 (October 8, 1969), pp. 58–59.

57. *Peking Review,* no. 35 (August 26, 1966), pp. 8–9.

58. Asia Research Center, *The Great Cultural Revolution in China* (Hong Kong: Asia Research Center, 1968), p. 422.

59. Hua-min Chung and Arthur C. Miller, *Madame Mao: A Profile of Chiang Ch'ing* (Hong Kong: Union Research Institute, 1968), p. 44.

60. Ibid., p. 71.

61. *Survey of China Mainland Press,* no. 3836 (December 8, 1966), pp. 1–2.

62. "Excerpts from Premier Chou En-lai's Comment on the Situation in Northeast China" (September 28, 1967), cited in Yu-shen Chien, *China's Fading Revolution: Army Dissent and Military Divisions, 1967–68* (Hong Kong: Center of Contemporary Chinese Studies, 1969), p. 319.

63. Karnow, op. cit., p. 169.

64. Chung and Miller, op. cit., p. 131.

65. Karnow, op. cit., p. 160.

66. Chien, op. cit., p. 138.

67. *Current Background,* no. 891 (October 8, 1969), p. 68.

68. *Peking Review,* no. 35 (August 26, 1966), p. 21.

69. *CCP Documents,* p. 72.

70. Ibid.

71. Ibid., p. 79.

72. Israel, op. cit., p. 13.

73. Jurgen Domes, *The Internal Politics of China 1949–1972* (New York: Praeger, 1973), p. 168.

74. *CCP Documents,* pp. 97–99.

75. *People's Daily,* September 11, 1966.

76. "Speech by Chou En-lai" (September 25, 1966); "Speech to Red Guard Representatives" (September 1, 1966), *Current Background,* no. 819 (March 10, 1967), p. 18.

77. *Survey of China Mainland Press,* no. 3785 (September 21, 1966), p. 4.

78. *The China Quarterly,* no. 29 (January/March 1967), p. 188.

79. *The Case of P'eng Teh-huai 1959–1968,* p. vi.

80. *Yomiuri* (Tokyo), December 29, 1966, in Karnow, op. cit., p. 235.

81. *People's Daily,* January 1, 1967.

82. Frederick C. Teiwes, *Provincial Leadership in China: The Cultural Revolution and Its Aftermath* (Ithaca, N.Y.: Cornell University China-Japan Program, 1974), p. 17.

83. Ibid., p. 5.

# 3

## MILITARY INTERVENTION
## AND REVOLUTIONARY COMMITTEES

As confusion and disorder spread in the wake of intramural fighting among rival Red Guard factions, and pitched battles continued between these young radicals and groups of workers and peasants organized to resist them, the Maoists realized that force would be necessary to maintain the radical offensive. Anticipating the use of the PLA, Lin Piao tightened his grip over the military by winnowing out dissident elements within its ranks. Ho Lung, legendary First Field Army hero and third-ranking MAC vice-chairman, was the first to fall in early January 1967.

Ho Lung was accused of sympathizing with pro-Liu Red Guard factions, as well as of committing many outrageous offenses dating as far back as World War II. According to Red Guard accounts, Ho had disparaged Mao's "wise statements" regarding the strategy and tactics of China in the war against Japan; his more serious error lay in "consistently" opposing the study of Mao Tse-tung's thought, which had been made compulsory by Lin Piao when Lin became minister of defense.[1] Reportedly, Ho had forbade his subordinates to follow this directive or ridiculed them for "studying nonsense."[2]

Factional relationships figured importantly in Ho's downfall. Ho allegedly had "maintained very close relations"[3] with P'eng Teh-huai, spurring P'eng on during his unsuccessful confrontation with Mao at the 1959 Lushan Plenum. Given the task in 1964 of criticizing P'eng Teh-huai, Ho had procrastinated as long as possible and then delivered a speech repudiating Huang K'o-cheng, thus shifting the target[4] of the attack in an attempt to "vindicate"[5] P'eng. In addition, Ho, P'eng Chen, and Teng Hsiao-p'ing were characterized as "jackals from the same lair."[6] P'eng Chen, regarded by Ho as one of his most admired Party leaders,[7] introduced Ho to his ninth wife, and quickly promoted her "4 grades in succession."[8] Ho secretly had sought P'eng's advice on matters within the jurisdiction of the MAC.[9] To Teng Hsiao-p'ing, whom he "adored" very much,[10] Ho owed a debt for bringing him to Peking as chairman of the Physical Culture Commission of the State Council.

The unforgivable sin as far as Lin Piao was concerned was that Ho had "consistently opposed and openly staged a rival show against vice chairman Lin Piao":

> When Vice Chairman Lin Piao was on sick leave, Ho Lung worked in collusion with Lo Jui-ch'ing to block him. Ho Lung never asked for instruction from Vice Chairman Lin Piao, and basically did not go to see him. In the past few years, many of Vice Chairman Lin Piao's important instructions were transmitted through other comrades of the General Staff and the General Political Department, and were seldom transmitted through Ho Lung and Lo Jui-ch'ing. Those instructions which were transmitted through Ho Lung and Lo Jui-ch'ing were either distorted or tampered with by them.[11]

Plotting "to usurp leadership in the army," Ho had cultivated his own coterie and placed these followers in strategic positions whenever possible. One such instance occurred when Ho "ousted Lai XX" and installed his nephew, Liao Han-sheng, as political commissar for the Peking MD:

> Through Liao, Ho stretched his sinister hand into the X Army; ... in the name of defending the Party CC and Chairman Mao they plotted to transfer the X Army under their control to Peking for the purpose of staging a coup.[12]

Ho's purge was accompanied by the downfall of many associates, a majority of whom had served in the First Field Army. They included Liao Han-sheng; Yang Yung, commander of the Peking MR; Su Chen-hua, political commissar of the navy; Liu Chen and Ch'eng Chün, deputy commanders of the air force; and Liu Chih-chien, deputy director of the PLA Cultural Revolution Group and deputy director of the PLA General Political Department. Others who also were removed, later in 1967, were Li Ching-ch'uan, who "formerly served under Ho" and whose "two sons were brought up in Ho's family"; and Huang Hsin-t'ing, commander of the Chengtu MR and "faithful lackey of Ho's."[13]

At the same time the Cultural Revolution Group of the PLA, probably created in October 1966 and first placed under the supervision of Liu Chih-chien, a close associate of Ho Lung, was reorganized on January 11, 1967. The CCRG, rather than the General Political Department of the PLA, was given jurisdiction over operations of the PLA Cultural Revolution Group, in conjunction with the MAC. And Hsü Hsiang-ch'ien, a semiretired marshal with Second and "Fifth" Field Army ties, became the group's new director. Also during January T'ao Chu fell from power; charged [Shao-ch'i] [Hsiao-p'ing] with being "a behind-the-scenes leader of the Liu-Teng line and also a two-faced false person" who had "carried out things in secrecy without inform-ing"[14] the CCRG, T'ao had allegedly tried "to strangle" the Cultural Revolution in Kwangtung province through a trusted supporter, Chao Tzu-yang. In a June 22, 1966, telephone conversation he had instructed Chao to "take advantage of this situation," to "appear in the 'Leftist' guise and seize power," and tell the students to follow the leadership of work teams and the provincial Party committee.[15]

Having eliminated some of their most formidable opponents, the Maoists convened an unexpected session of the MAC on January 20–21, 1967. On the following day, *People's Daily* published an order reportedly issued at the command of Mao:

> The revolutionary masses . . . clench their teeth and, with steel-like determi-nation, make up their mind to unite, form a great alliance, seize power! Seize power!! Seize power!!! All the Party power, political power and financial power usurped by the counter-revolutionary revisionists and those diehards who persistently cling to the bourgeois reactionary line must be recaptured! . . . If the enemy refuses to surrender, we will finish him off![16]

On January 23, 1967, the MAC, reversing its earlier decision to avoid the use of the PLA in the Cultural Revolution, issued a secret order:

> 1. All the earlier orders that the armed forces should not intervene in the Cultural Revolution should be regarded as void.
> 2. The PLA should actively support the power seizure of the revolution-ary leftists and masses. Troops should be sent to render active assistance when requested by the genuine proletarian leftists.
> 3. Sternly suppress the anti-revolutionary elements and organizations if they oppose the proletarian leftists. If they use force, the PLA should return fire determinedly.
> 4. The PLA should not become a shelter for the minority in the Party who have taken the capitalist road and those who insist on the capitalist, reaction-ary line.
> 5. Carry out deeply within the Army the proletarian revolutionary line represented by Chairman Mao and struggle against the reactionary capitalist line led by Liu Shao-ch'i and Teng Hsiao-p'ing.[17]

The order was related "word for word to every PLA soldier," and the *Liberation Army Daily,* immediately voicing its support of the new assignment, declared on January 24:

> We swear to be the powerful shield of the proletarian revolutionary rebels and to support the struggle of the revolutionary rebels to take power.[18]

Large segments of the PLA were dispatched to various areas to carry out their mission of "three supports and two militaries"—to support the leftists, industry, and agriculture and to implement military control and training.

## "THREE SUPPORTS AND TWO MILITARIES"

### "Support Leftists"

The PLA's first and major obligation was to "support the leftists" under the supervision of the "Support-leftists Headquarters" of the MD or PLA forces stationed in the local areas. They were to provide moral and material assistance to groups they judged to be true leftists in the fighting that frequently marked confrontations between radicals and their opponents, and at the same time attempt to maintain order in the community as best they could.

### "Support Industry"

When PLA units arrived at a factory on their mission "to support industry," they mediated between the intruding Red Guards and workers eager to protect their special privileges as well as among rival worker cliques to prevent further escalation of the violent fighting. To win over workers and arouse their enthusiasm, the military eliminated some of the existing unpopular regulations and measures. Meanwhile, they conducted propaganda activities through newly organized Mao Tse-tung Thought study classes as part of the "struggle-criticism-transformation" campaign to reform errant workers. Finally, many PLA units were dispatched to factories to accelerate production by laboring alongside the workers, the CC acknowledged in "A Letter to Revolutionary Cadres and Workers of Mining and Industrial Enterprises."[19] Thus, some PLA soldiers participated in factory work for one or two days a week, but most were assigned as regular workers.

### "Support Agriculture"

Commanders of MDs established special departments "to support agriculture," and sent troops to villages and communes where the economy of the collectives had been disrupted by the excesses of the Cultural Revolution and spring planting delayed. In "A Letter to the Cadres, Poor and Lower-Middle Peasants of the People's Communes,"[20] the CC urged the PLA to help out as much as possible with the necessary work on the communes. It was reported, for example, that the Nanking 610th, stationed in Anhwei province, organized a "support-left" column to assist the peasants in spring planting in nearby *hsiens* such as Lu-an and Chin-chai,[21] and an artillery unit of the same corps worked with more than one hundred production brigades in their locality.[22]

In addition, Mao Tse-tung's Thought Propaganda Teams were dispatched to communes and production brigades as they had been to factories to "raise the consciousness" of the peasants and in particular to correct the "bourgeois" practices of falsifying records of production, illegally dividing public storages, cultivating private lots at the expense of commune farming, and so on. Lanchow troops, for instance, boasted of having sent more than 15,000 men in 500 "teams" to 110 *hsiens* for this purpose.[23]

## "Military Control"

The PLA was authorized to take over any government or Party organization where factional strife had disrupted its administrative capacity or threatened its existence. The first reported case of "military control" occurred on February 11, 1967, in Peking,[24] where the Peking Garrison put the people's police and public security organs under their jurisdiction. Soon afterwards, a Military Control Commission was formed under the tutelage of local military forces to assume the functions of the defunct Party and government apparatus, a pattern repeated in other provinces both at the provincial and local levels.

## "Military Training"

The PLA was authorized, in its mission of "military training," to send troops to upper elementary schools, high schools, universities, and colleges to maintain order when factional fighting among rival student groups persisted, as well as to conduct ideological reforms similar to those in agriculture and industry. One example was the "Peking Garrison General Headquarters for Military Training," which sent troops to 385 middle schools, 834 elementary schools, and "several" universities in the Peking area, involving more than one million teachers and students.[25]

The achievements of the PLA in restoring order on many campuses were widely acclaimed. At the celebration of the establishment of its revolutionary committee (RC) on September 27, 1969, Peking University admitted that "situations at Peita quickly changed during the past year, especially after the stationing of the 'support-left' units of the PLA 8341 troops."[26] In some cases, Mao Tse-tung Thought Propaganda Teams, composed of workers under the guidance of PLA political advisers, were dispatched to various campuses. When one of these teams successfully negotiated a truce between conflicting factions at Tsinghua University in July 1968, Mao urged that more teams of this type be sent to all schools for an extended stay in order to supervise the operations of the schools. The PLA was ordered to support these worker groups "wholeheartedly."[27]

Necessitated by national disorder unforeseen by the central authorities when the Red Guards were unleashed, the "three-supports-two-militaries" decision marked the beginning of overt military intervention in the political and economic life of the People's Republic, posing new problems to the reestablishment of central authority.

## Clashes between the Military and the Leftists

When the military began moving into troubled areas, they placed under their jurisdiction local police and public security personnel[28] in the name of Military Control Commissions that exercised total control over the local population.[29] But like so many other decisions made by the Party center, this action ran into many unanticipated difficulties.

Since the multitude of Red Guard groups and mass organizations all claimed to be the true supporters of Mao and many "waved the red flag to oppose the red flag," it was not easy for the PLA to determine which group was genuinely leftist, and they often dragged their feet for fear of having chosen the wrong side. Scattered reports indicate that some units of the PLA did indeed commit such errors. The confusion was exacerbated by the Red Guards' sometimes indiscriminate attacks on the military, even those friendly to their cause. For example, Ch'en Tsai-tao, commander of the Wuhan MR, said during his trial for having supported the wrong Red Guard group, "They bugged our troops day after day," adding angrily, "What kind of prick revolutionaries are they?"[30] Some PLA units, unsympathetic to any contending group, adopted a neutral posture and decided, to the consternation of all, to "look on with folded arms and to sit on the hill to watch the tigers fight."[31] It also was apparent that a few local military commanders were more concerned with maintaining order and stability than with assisting the leftists to overthrow the local Party apparatus, arguing that "we would draw fire to our door, get us into trouble, and thus affect the stability of our troops."[32] Worse still, some PLA units shared the views of the rightists and therefore "prevented the transmission of directives of the Central Committee to the lower levels" or came to the rightists' defense.[33]

By early March 1967, reports that local military commanders were taking advantage of their new authority by vigorously cracking down on the Red Guards and other disorderly youths became distressingly frequent. The Military Control Commission in Anhwei, for example, was said to have arrested radicals "indiscriminately" and "monopolized" local authority.

## THE "FEBRUARY ADVERSE CURRENT"

From the civilian sector also came a challenge to the onslaught of the leftists—the so-called "February Adverse Current." In the spring of 1967, members of this movement

> ... wildly supported the bourgeois reactionary line, in a vain attempt to overthrow the proletarian headquarters led by Chairman Mao as the supreme commander and Vice-chairman Lin as the deputy supreme commander, to overthrow the Central Cultural Revolution Group which held high the great red banner of Mao Tse-tung's thought, and to reverse the verdict on China's Khrushchev and other top Party persons in authority taking the capitalist road. ...[34]

Chiang Ch'ing identified the leaders of this movement as T'an Chen-lin and Yu Ch'iu-li.[35] T'an, a vice-premier of the State Council and Politburo member whose closeness to Teng Hsiao-p'ing, Ho Lung, and Chen Yi was well known,[36] was accused of "persistently opposing Chairman Mao and Vice-chairman Lin" and "attempting to destroy the unity of the PLA and the foundation of the new-born Revolutionary Committees."[37] Chiang declared:

> T'an Chen-lin is a renegade. I used to protect him. Now I must shout: 'Down with T'an Chen-lin! Down with T'an Chen-lin!' He is a black fighter of Liu, Teng [Hsiao-p'ing] and T'ao [Chu]. We now have conclusive evidence against him. He is a renegade.[38]

In a speech on March 27, 1968, Chiang charged Yu Ch'iu-li, the minister of petroleum of the State Council, of being "a close confidante of Ho Lung."[39] According to her, "Chairman Mao said that he [Yu] should be 'criticized first and then protected,' but he [T'an] would not criticize him." What actually happened, Chiang said, was that "they [T'an and his supporters] said: 'Who-[ever] opposes Yu Ch'iu-li, XX and XX [also] opposes the premier and Chairman Mao.' This is confusing black and white."[40]

## Curbs on the Military

Alarmed that the army had subverted the original purpose of its assignment and was now undermining the goals of the Cultural Revolution, the Maoists at the center cautioned that despite the shortcomings or errors on the part of the leftists, they should be given full weight and their opinions heeded.[41] Further, the Party central sent out investigative teams to localities where the Red Guards had suffered the most severe persecution.

But the army, by now entrenched in their position of power, enjoyed their newly acquired authority and proved unresponsive to the commands of the center. As the suppression of the Red Guards continued, on April 1, 1967, the Maoists adopted the first measure to curtail the authority of the army. While retaining responsibility for the maintenance of order and the establishment of RCs where they were stationed, the army was forbidden to indict, without prior approval from central authorities, any Red Guard faction for being "counter-revolutionary"[42] and was ordered to release all imprisoned radicals, including those who had raided military installations. The military was further instructed not to overreact or suppress the radicals under the pretext of "suppressing counter-revolution" after having forced them to admit guilt.[43] Reaffirming the infallibility of the masses, this directive declared:

> Chairman Mao has more than once taught us that 'it is not a crime to make revolution,' 'it is not a crime to speak out,' and 'it is not a crime to practice extensive democracy.' To force the masses to admit guilt is extremely wrong. Suppression of the revolutionary masses under the pretext of 'suppressing counter-revolution' is strictly forbidden.[44]

Among the many critics of the army, Chiang Ch'ing was by far the most vociferous. Speaking to a group of Red Guards in Peking on April 4, she reproached the PLA for persecuting the radicals, emphasized the "duty" of the army to "support the left," and urged the military to "respect the Red Guards and other representatives of the masses" and to "join with them in the construction of new revolutionary power structure to replace the shattered Party administration."[45]

Some time in early April, Hsu Hsiang-ch'ien, the head of the Cultural Revolution Group in the army, was dismissed when this group was reorganized for the second time, presumably because of his overly protective attitude toward the armed forces. Many local PLA commanders began to be attacked in wall posters. Hsu was replaced by Hsiao Hua, a close associate of Lin Piao and head of the General Political Department of the PLA. Hsiao Hua now warned of possible purges to eliminate the "small handful" who advocated the "bourgeois reactionary line"[46] in the military and forbade soldiers to use force even in self-defense.

## Return to the Radicals

Encouraged by the new constraints on the army and exhilarated by fresh encouragement from the Maoists at the center, the Red Guards and other young militants resumed their violent struggle, looting ammunition depots for weapons and renewing their assaults on the local military establishment. Confused and angered by the conflicting directives from Peking, local army commanders took matters into their own hands and fought back in self-defense. In late spring of 1967, nearly every region of China experienced widespread, devastating disorders. The country was engulfed in what the newspapers later called "unprincipled civil wars" and "sheer anarchy."[47]

The Party, faced with a grave threat to the country's stability, was forced to counter the disruption caused by the Red Guards by issuing a new directive on June 6 forbidding them "to make arrests" and "to set up courts"; to seize or destroy official documents or files; to "occupy, smash or seize" properties of the State ; or "to carry on sabotage under any pretext." Furthermore, they were "strictly prohibited to carry on armed struggle, to beat up people, to fight in groups in one's own unit or in larger units, or to rob properties belonging to individuals."[48]

The directive reminded the local military forces of their responsibility in maintaining law and order but failed to grant them permission to use force against disruptive groups and individuals.[49] Local military commanders had to assume full responsibility for their actions, and thus became understandably hesitant in taking any action which might antagonize the Maoists in Peking.

As the situation at the regional and local levels continued to deteriorate and as the country verged on total collapse, the Chinese leadership met in early summer 1967 to search for a desperately needed solution to the nation's mounting problems. By now the fundamental differences between Chou En-lai and Chiang Ch'ing could no longer be camouflaged. Supported by regional military commanders, Chou argued for renewed military suppression of disruptive elements, while Chiang Ch'ing and other radicals firmly opposed such a move. They eventually compromised and reached a decision to dispatch high-level delegations to the troubled areas. These delegations were to determine which group was genuinely revolutionary, thus deserving support, and at the same time act as conciliators in an effort to end factional fighting. One delegation was headed by Hsieh Fu-chih and Wang Li, who, as personal envoys of Mao Tse-tung, left Peking in July for Yunnan and Hupeh provinces, where fighting had been most intense.

## The Wuhan Incident: The Military Rebellion against the Leftists

In the industrial city of Wuhan in Hupeh province, two factions had been at each other's throats for months. One, known as the "One Million Heroes," was composed mostly of a half-million workers, militiamen, and party cadres and was backed by the regional military commander, Ch'en Tsai-tao, first appointed to his post in 1954 and a close associate of T'ao Chu. Its rival, the "Workers Headquarters," consisted of local workers favoring the radical cause led by Red Guards from Peking. Numerically inferior, it, too, received military backing but from units disloyal to Ch'en. Fierce fighting broke out several times between these two groups, resulting in hundreds of casualties. Hoping to negotiate a truce, Hsieh Fu-chih and Wang Li arrived in Wuhan on July 14, 1967. After having consulted both factions, they decided that Ch'en had erred in supporting the "One Million Heroes." Some of Ch'en's supporters refused to accept this verdict and kidnapped the two envoys, who were then beaten before being released.

Their mistreatment represented an open defiance of Mao and the central authorities. Lin Piao himself went to Wuhan to mount the offensive against Ch'en. Gunboats and paratroopers took part in the assault, and the city was taken by government forces in late July. Ch'en and some of his supporters were captured and brought to Peking for trial. Ch'en's unsuccessful effort to challenge the central authority, nevertheless, touched off another spasm of fighting between radical groups and local military units in many parts of the country.

## The "May 16th Corps": The Purge of the Extreme Leftists

Citing the Wuhan incident as evidence of the military's antagonism toward the goals of the Cultural Revolution, the leftists in Peking renewed their demand to purge "the small handful of those in authority in the Army who take the capitalist road."[50] A small minority, the "May 16th Corps," who were later labeled extreme leftists, even advocated the arming of the Red Guards. With the support of Chiang Ch'ing, Ch'en Po-ta urged the Red Guards to prepare for "protracted war," because the exchange "of a few words"[51] would not resolve the deep-rooted conflict. In early August 1967 Lin Piao declared at a conference of high-echelon PLA cadres, "We should obey Chairman Mao's directive, arm the leftists, and give guns to the left masses."[52] The radicals then promptly acquired weapons by any means possible: raiding arsenals, looting Soviet supplies en route to North Vietnam, or ambushing their opposition. To counter such grave threats, the military equipped their sympathizers with an uninterrupted flow of materials and provided operational guidance. Since all claimed to be genuine revolutionaries and therefore were entitled to use force, the level of fighting that broke out in almost every province was unprecedented. It is no exaggeration to state that August of 1967 represented the most violent, bloody phase of the Cultural Revolution.

During August, Chou En-lai and the State Council came under attack by the "May 16th Corps," which had long been disenchanted with Chou's moderate policies. Ch'en Yi, the minister of foreign affairs, former Third Field Army leader and close friend of Chou En-lai, was again confronted with a round of severe, prolonged criticism. A blunt, outspoken man, Ch'en, it was widely known, held Chiang Ch'ing's dramas in low esteem and pointed out that they attracted no audience, saying, "There is no question about ideology, but there will be no plays."[53] At times he argued with Chiang so heatedly that their faces would "turn red."[54] Furthermore, Ch'en felt that Liu Shao-ch'i had been punished excessively and defended Chu Teh and Ho Lung: "I have opposed Chairman Mao on several occasions in the past, and I am not quite sure I won't do so in the future."[55] In March he had rehabilitated some ministry officials who earlier had been attacked and with the help of Liao Ch'eng-chih, chairman of the Overseas Chinese Affairs Commission, engineered "sham power seizures" by friendly rebels in the Foreign Affairs Ministry. In April Ch'en Yi, under heavy attack, was temporarily relieved of his ministry duties, and Ch'en Po-ta reported that Chou En-lai took over for a time.

However, on August 7, 1967, Wang Li, a leading spokesman of the "May 16th Corps," broadly hinted at a meeting of ministry personnel that Mao had instructed him to assume control of the ministry. With the slogans "doubting all" and "overthrowing all,"[56] Wang and his supporters invaded the ministry for two weeks in August, then appointed Yao Teng-shan, a former charge d'affaires in Indonesia, as Ch'en Yi's replacement.[57] On August 22, the Corps continued its rampage by burning down the British Embassy in Peking and harassing its personnel as well as other foreign diplomats.

Military leaders, especially regional commanders, disgusted with the excesses committed by the extreme leftists, made known their determination not to tolerate such bizarre behavior any longer and exerted pressure on the CCRG through Lin Piao. As a result, Wang Li, a member of the CCRG, was accused of "leading and organizing"[58] the "May 16th Corps," then arrested in late August 1967 as an "agent of the Kuomintang (KMT)."[59] Shortly thereafter, more members of the corps fell; accused of being principal participants and subsequently arrested were other members of the CCRG, Lin Chieh, Kuan Feng, and Mu Hsin. In March of 1968, an additional CCRG member, Ch'i Pen-yu, branded a "counter-revolutionary" posing as a "leftist"[60] and charged with "counter-revolutionary double dealing,"[61] was dismissed. The "May 16th Corps" was condemned as "left in form but right in substance."[62]

When the "May 16th Corps" fell, Chiang Ch'ing, surprisingly enough, was the first to attack these radicals. In a speech delivered on September 5, 1967, she denied that she had ever advocated violence:

> Comrades, I am not in favor of armed struggle, and you must not think that I like it, because I am firmly opposed to it. I resolutely support Chairman Mao's call for 'peaceful struggle, not armed struggle.' What I mean is when the class enemies attack us, how can we afford not to have an inch of iron in our hands? This is the situation I have in mind, but at present we need not have that kind of armed struggle.[63]

Then Chiang denounced the ultraleftists:

At present, let us take Peking as an example. There is a bad thing, and I call it a bad thing because it is a counterrevolutionary organization called the 'May 16th Corps.' Numerically, it is not a large organization, and superficially, the majority of its members are young people, who are actually the hoodwinked. The minority consists of bourgeois elements who nurse deep-seated hatred for us and who make use of the ideological instability of the young people. Those who really pull strings behind the scene are very bad indeed.

The May 16th assumes an ultra-leftist appearance; it centers its opposition on the Premier. Actually, it has collected black materials to denounce every one of us, and it may throw it out in public at any time. . . . The May 16th is a very typical counterrevolutionary organization and we must raise our vigilance against it.[64]

Despite her efforts to disassociate herself, Chiang, nevertheless, still suffered a temporary diminution of power as the radicals fell from grace, for her ties with this group were known to all. Mao forced both Chiang Ch'ing and Ch'en Po-ta to undergo self-criticism and confess leftist-opportunistic errors.[65]

The excesses committed by the "May 16th Corps" and the unremitting attacks on local military prompted Mao to make this statement in late August 1967:

The army's prestige must be resolutely safeguarded and there can be no doubt whatever about that. Publication of editorials on the need to support the army and cherish the people is the center of the work. It is unavoidable that the army should have made mistakes in tackling for the first time the large-scale fighting task of supporting the left, supporting industry and agriculture, and carrying out military control and military training. The chief danger of the moment is that some people want to beat down the People's Liberation Army. . . . There must be no chaos in the army.[66]

Chiang Ch'ing, a steadfast supporter of the radical cause who on July 22 had advocated arming the Red Guards in order to defend the purity of the Cultural Revolution "by force"[67] if necessary, had changed her opinion by September 1967:

Sometime earlier, there was this wrong slogan: Seize a 'small handful in the army.' As a result, 'a small handful in the army' was seized everywhere and even the weapons of our regular troops were seized. . . . Comrades, come to think of it: Without the People's Liberation Army, is it possible for us to sit in the People's Great Hall holding a conference? (The audience: No.) If our field armies were thrown into confusion and if trouble occurred, could we tolerate such a situation? (The audience: No.) Let us not fall into the trap. The slogan is wrong. Because the Party, the government and the army are

all under the leadership of the Party. We can only talk about dragging out
the handful of Party capitalist roaders in authority and nothing else.[68]

Chou concurred:

'Drag out the handful from the Army,' which was recently put forward, is
an erroneous slogan and has adversely affected some localities. We have
talked to all concerned and corrected it by discarding 'Drag out the handful
from the Army.' That, however, does not mean that there are no mistakes
in our Army. Individuals in the People's Liberation Army have made mistakes and even very serious ones or committed crimes.[69]

Chiang was credited by Chou as being the first person to expose members of
the "May 16th Corps," "a great achievement of the Central Cultural Revolution Group and Comrade Chiang Ch'ing."[70]

Nevertheless, anarchy persisted, and Peking had no alternative except to
order the army to intervene once again. On September 5, 1967, the army was
authorized for the first time in the Cultural Revolution to open fire against
unruly "mass organizations or individuals" who "resist arrest or fight back."[71]
From September onward, the PLA responded vigorously and moved in to fill
the power vacuum.

At the end of 1967, only 6 of the original 13 members of the CCRG were
still active, and at the local level, the radicals had been similarly excluded from
positions of authority. Voicing their disillusion in "Whither China?", an essay
written in January 1968, the radicals protested that "everything remains the
same after so much ado," since "the form of political power has only superficially changed. The old Party committee and the old Military District have
become the Revolutionary Committee [and] old bureaucrats continue to play
the leading role."[72] They added that although the masses had managed to gain
control of the country during January 1967, the old establishment had suppressed them "by the most urgent and savage means"; that Premier Chou, the
"general representative of China's red capitalist class," had engineered this
"counter-revolutionary" coup; and furthermore, that the army had been
Chou's willing accomplice in imposing the "new bourgeois dictatorship"[73] on
China through the creation of RCs.

## The Leftists Rebound

By early 1968 the leftists persuaded the Party leadership that the correc-
tive measures so far implemented had become excessive and that whatever the
cost, the goals of the Cultural Revolution should not be abandoned. In a series
of speeches Chiang Ch'ing warned in March that conservatives still constituted

the "main danger throughout the country" and said, "We must take the class stand firmly and heighten our vigilance."[74]

In a measure designed to placate the Maoists, three senior military officers —Yang Ch'eng-wu, Fu Ch'ung-pi, and Yu Li-chin—were purged. On March 22 in Peking, where Lin Piao and Mao received more than 10,000 PLA commanders from the regimental level and above,[75] Lin announced the dismissal of Yang Ch'eng-wu, the acting chief of staff, who was accused of "install[ing] bugging devices in Mao's residence and office in his plot to overthrow the Chairman"[76] and of employing "secret police methods" to compile a dossier of "black materials"[77] on Chou En-lai and Chiang Ch'ing to incriminate them. He was also charged with helping Fu Ch'ung-pi, the commander of Peking Garrison Force, "to crash into the headquarters of CCRG on March 8 . . . [as they] attempted to arrest some of its members."[78] As if she had been waiting for their intrusion, Chiang Ch'ing reportedly

> then came forward and agrily scolded Fu the scab. The latter, believing he had Yang Ch'eng-wu's backing, went so far as to retort and hurl abuses at Comrade Chiang Ch'ing.[79]

Yang was called a "two-faced and ambitious careerist," and Fu shared Yang's criminal designation of a "right-wing splitist."[80] Ousted also was Yu Li-chin, the political commissar of the air force, for being a "rebel" who had committed "extremely grave mistakes."[81] To what extent the offenses committed by Yang and his comrades can be substantiated remains in doubt; however, all three had been in the forefront of the army's efforts to subdue the Red Guards, and, explaining their fall in an April 7, 1968, speech to the State Planning Commission, Chou said:

> The February [1967] Adverse Current, with T'an Chen-lin as its representative, appeared and many people joined in cheering it. In many ministries and provinces were found those who attempted to reverse the verdict on the 'capitalist-roaders.' That is why we carried out criticisms against this group last February to May. In May and June, the extreme 'left' rose and created much commotion, particularly during July and August. However, after our Chairman issued his directive, the 'right' rebounded in October, and Yang, Fu and Yu overstepped their bounds.[82]

Despite the ouster of Yang, Fu, and Yu, the fate of the Red Guards had already been sealed by the middle of 1968. Mao said of them in his "Eighteen-Point Instruction:"

> When we do things, some people have to assume command. Can the Red Guards assume command? They will certainly be toppled tomorrow once they are installed today. This is because they are politically immature. . . .

The Red Guards are incompetent; they haven't been tempered. We can't trust them with things of such major importance.[83]

The demise of the Red Guards did not mean that the PLA was given a free rein to govern. The Party central was determined to impose tighter discipline. Local military cadres were summoned to Peking for a series of "study classes," which, though beginning in the fall of 1967, did not reach a peak until mid-1968 as "hundreds of thousands of PLA personnel" received such a "re-education."[84] Yet some military personnel remained troublesome, a fact Chou En-lai acknowledged in a July 25, 1968, speech:

Now you comrades are invited to Peking and to the side of Chairman Mao, to study the thought of Mao Tse-tung and Chairman Mao's revolutionary line. Most of the comrades have come, but a few are unwilling to come to the side of Chairman, to the Mao Tse-tung's thought study class set up by the Central Committee. Then there are some who, though they have come to Peking, have not come to the study class, but are carrying out activities in underground sewers.[85]

Chou assailed those who continued to exert pressure whenever they could as they had done before:

If you comrades have any ideas, you may speak out. The Central Committee is democratic-minded. But I have to tell you that you are not here to argue a case. You cannot insist on conditions, and, what's more, you cannot insist on bargaining with the proletarian headquarters headed by Chairman Mao and with Vice-chairman Lin as deputy. You have come here to study the thought of Mao Tse-tung and Chairman Mao's revolutionary line. It won't do for you to bargain with the proletarian headquarters! This is a meeting called by the Central Committee. If you bargain here, what will the Central Committee do? Will the Central Committee obey you, or you the Central Committee?[86]

## THE REVOLUTIONARY COMMITTEES: A COALITION

In every province where the PLA successfully subdued all opposition, a "Revolutionary Committee" was created to assume the duties and functions ordinarily performed by the Party organization and local government administration, as the following notice, issued by the Heilungkiang Provincial RC, revealed:

All the organizations under the former Provincial Chinese Communist Party Committee and the Provincial People's Council are hereby declared abol-

ished. All their functions shall be gradually handed over to the Provincial
Revolutionary Committee with the help of the take-over committees of the
respective organizations. All these take-over committees shall tentatively be
under the leadership of the Provincial Revolutionary Committee. All notices
issued by the subordinate units, whenever concerned with important policy
or line, shall be submitted to the Provincial Revolutionary Committee for
approval; without approval they are null and void.[87]

The Heilungkiang RC, established on January 31, 1967, was the first of
29 provincial units to be formed, and the last was created in the Sinkiang
Uighur Autonomous Region (AR) on September 5, 1968. The RC did more
than provide an opportunity to discard Party rule—they ushered in a new elite.
Of the 29 who were first Party secretaries in the provincial and municipal Party
committees, only one, Chang Kuo-hua, became the chairman of an RC, and
none of the 21 previous provincial governors or three mayors of the centrally
directed cities was so honored. One chairman in the five ARs, Wei Kuo-ch'ing,
managed to become the chairman of his region's newly created RC, but he was
definitely an exception.

The RCs were to be organized on the basis of the "triple alliance," known
also as the "three-in-one combination" or "three-way alliance." The Heilungkiang RC, cited as a "good example" of the new governing unit by *People's
Daily,* proclaimed:

> Only by means of this 'three-in-one' combination can we form a truly great
> alliance of proletarian revolution; only so can we truly seize Party, political,
> financial and cultural powers from the handful of persons who are in author-
> ity and taking the capitalist road, consolidate political power and win com-
> plete victory in the struggle to seize power.[88]

*Red Flag* urged:

> . . . [I]n those places and organizations where power needs to be seized, the
> policy of the revolutionary 'three-in-one' combination must be carried out
> in establishing a provisional organ of power that is revolutionary and repre-
> sentative and has proletarian authority.[89]

The "triple alliance" amounted to an ingenious formula of coalition designed
to accommodate all the major rival groups by distributing representation
among the PLA; "revolutionary cadres" who were pro-Mao Party members
during the Cultural Revolution; and the vaguely defined "revolutionary
rebels" consisting mainly of activists who had battled against the Liu faction.

The participation of the PLA in the "three-in-one combination" was
justified because they had "played an extremely important role in successfully
accomplishing the task in the struggle to seize power,"[90] and they were "an

extremely revolutionary army of the proletariat," [whose] "sole purpose" was "to stand firmly with the Chinese people and to serve them wholeheartedly."[91] Revolutionary cadres were included since they were "more mature politically. They have greater organizational skill. They are more experienced in struggle. They have the ability to exercise power and administer work for the state of the proletariat."[92] In conformity with the Party's emphasis on the "mass line," the importance of the "revolutionary rebel" groups was stressed because they were the "representatives of the broad revolutionary masses."[93] And "the masses," as Mao frequently pointed out, "are the real heroes . . . [with] boundless creative power . . . [who] are the motive force in the making of world history."[94]

Officially, all three groups were "equally indispensable"[95] and "it was wrong to overlook or underestimate the functions of any one group,"[96] but in reality the military obviously dominated these bodies with the exception of Shanghai, as Table 1 shows.

Of the 29 initial chairmen of the RCs, 22 were from unmistakably military origins, most having served as PLA officers or political commissars.[97] The remaining seven chairmen could be categorized as "revolutionary cadres."[98] More significantly, "revolutionary rebels," while occupying 88 of 203 vice-chairmanships, failed to achieve even one chairmanship in an RC despite repeated official proclamations that the leaders of mass organizations "must not be taken as second-fiddle players,"[99] and that:

## TABLE 1
### Composition of the Revolutionary Committees

| | Position | | |
| | Chairman | Vice-Chairman | Total |
| --- | --- | --- | --- |
| PLA | | | |
| Number | 22 | 60 | 82 |
| Percent | 75.8 | 29.5 | 35.3 |
| Cadres | | | |
| Number | 7 | 55 | 62 |
| Percent | 24.1 | 27.0 | 26.7 |
| Masses | | | |
| Number | 0 | 88 | 88 |
| Percent | 0 | 43.3 | 37.9 |
| TOTAL | 29 | 203 | 232 |

*Source:* Based on data from *Chung-kung yen-chiu, Chung-kung nien-pao*, and *Fei-ch'ing yueh-pao.*

If their role is not recognized or if it is underrated, in effect, the revolutionary masses as well as the Great Proletarian Cultural Revolution, are negated. If they are excluded or regarded as secondary, it is impossible to establish a provisional organ of power that is revolutionary, representative and has proletarian authority.[100]

It was obvious by now that central authorities and local ruling elites disagreed over who should govern.

## THE TWELFTH PLENUM AND THE OUSTER OF LIU SHAO-CH'I

With the creation of all provincial-level RCs and the gradual restoration of stability in most parts of the country, the Maoists felt sufficiently secure to deliver the final coup de grace to Liu Shao-ch'i. This occurred at the enlarged, Twelfth Plenum of the Eighth CC, held from October 13 to 31, 1968, and attended not only by members of the CC but also by "principal responsible comrades"[101] of the RCs and the PLA (purposely invited by the Maoists to lend support to the radical cause); the special group appointed by the CC to investigate Liu made its report, which was subsequently ratified by the plenum.

The report was a malicious exaggeration of Liu's alleged misconduct over the years. Among the accusations were that Liu had defected to Chao Heng-t'i, the Kuomintang governor of Hunan province, when he faced the death penalty after being arrested in Changsha in 1925; that Liu had sold out the interests of the working class and undermined the revolution by serving as a lackey to the Nationalist reactionaries Wang Ching-wei and Ch'en Kung-po at Wuhan in 1927; and that he secretly served the Manchurian warlord Chang Hsueh-liang in 1929, betraying the CCP underground.[102] Liu's ultimate crimes were that he had married in 1947 Wang Kuang-mei, "a U.S. agent sent to Yenan by the U.S. Strategic Information Service,"[103] and in 1959 had sent his brother-in-law, Wang Kuang-ch'i, to Hong Kong to supply "the U.S. Central Intelligence Agency with much information 'of high value which was highly regarded by the Americans.' "[104]

A plenum communique announced that the report

confirms with full supporting evidence that Liu Shao-ch'i, the No. 1 Party person in authority taking the capitalist road, is a renegade, traitor and scab hiding in the Party and is a lackey of imperialism, modern revisionism and the Kuomintang reactionaries who has committed innumerable crimes.[105]

Concluding the "Liu Shao-ch'i's crimes are so monstrous and extreme that death is too good for him,"[106] the report recommended that Liu be "expelled from the Party once and for all"[107] and dismissed from all his Party and state positions. The Party was urged to "continue to settle accounts with him and his accomplices for their crimes in betraying the Party and the country."[108]

To legitimize the expulsion of Liu from the CCP, a national Party congress had to be convened as soon as possible to comply with Article 16 of the 1956 Party Constitution:

> Any decision to remove a member or alternate member of the Central Committee of the Party from the Central Committee, to place him on probation or to expel him from the Party must be taken by the National Party Congress. In conditions of urgency, such decisions may be taken by a two-thirds majority vote of the Central Committee at its plenary session, but it must be subject to subsequent confirmation by the next session of the National Party Congress.[109]

The congress also was necessary to replace the purged Liuists in the CCP with Mao's supporters. The Twelfth Plenum, as part of its preparation for the event, adopted the draft of a revised party constitution written under the supervision of Ch'en Po-ta, Chang Ch'un-ch'iao, and Yao Wen-yuan.[110]

## NOTES

1. *Current Background,* no. 859 (January 20, 1967), p. 1.
2. *Survey of China Mainland Press,* no. 3912 (January 28, 1967), p. 10.
3. Ibid., p. 12.
4. *Current Background,* no. 859 (August 8, 1968), p. 36.
5. *Survey of China Mainland Press,* no. 3912, p. 12.
6. *Current Background,* no. 859, p. 1.
7. Ibid., p. 4.
8. Ibid., p. 36.
9. *Survey of China Mainland Press,* no. 3912, p. 11.
10. *Current Background,* no. 859, p. 35.
11. Ibid., p. 2.
12. Ibid., pp. 3–4.
13. Ibid.
14. Edward E. Rice, *Mao's Way* (Berkeley: University of California Press, 1972), p. 302.
15. *Survey of China Mainland Press,* no. 3935 (February 27, 1967), p. 14.
16. *People's Daily,* January 22, 1967.
17. Institute for the Study of Chinese Communist Problems, *Important CCP Documents of the Great Proletarian Cultural Revolution* (Taipei: Institute for the Study of Chinese Communist Problems, 1973) (hereafter, *Important CCP Documents*), p. 64.
18. *People's Daily,* January 24, 1967.
19. "Letter from the Central Committee of the Chinese Communist Party to Revolutionary Workers and Staff in Industrial and Mining Enterprises Throughout the Country" (March 18, 1967), *Peking Review,* no. 13 (March 24, 1967), pp. 5–6.
20. "A Letter to Poor and Lower-Middle Peasants and Cadres at All Levels in Rural People's Communes All Over the Country," *Peking Review,* no. 9 (February 24, 1967), p. 6.

21. Institute for the Study of Chinese Communist Problems, *1971 Chung-Kung nien-pao (Yearbook on Chinese Communism)* (Taipei: Institute for the Study of Chinese Communist Problems, 1971), p. 2:85.

22. Ibid.

23. Institute for the Study of Chinese Communist Problems, *1969 Yearbook on Chinese Communism* (Taipei: Institute for the Study of Chinese Communist Problems, 1969), p. 2:36.

24. Asia Research Center, *The Great Power Struggle in China* (Hong Kong: Asia Research Center, 1969), pp. 337–38.

25. *People's Daily,* March 7, 1968.

26. Institute for the Study of Chinese Communist Problems, *1970 Yearbook on Chinese Communism* (Taipei: Institute for the Study of Chinese Communist Problems, 1970), p. 2:90.

27. Institute for the Study of Chinese Communist Problems, *1969 Yearbook on Chinese Communism* (Taipei: Institute for the Study of Chinese Communist Problems, 1969), p. 2:38.

28. Institute for the Study of Chinese Communist Problems, *1968 Yearbook on Chinese Communism* (Taipei: Institute for the Study of Chinese Communist Problems, 1968) (hereafter, *1968 Yearbook*), p. 96.

29. Ibid.

30. *Important CCP Documents,* p. 406; see also *Survey of China Mainland Press,* no. 4089 (December 29, 1967), p. 11.

31. *Survey of China Mainland Magazines,* no. 567 (March 13, 1967), p. 2.

32. Ibid.

33. "Excerpts from Premier Chou En-lai's Comment on the Situation in Northeast China" (September 28, 1967), cited in Yu-shen Chien, *China's Fading Revolution: Army Dissent and Military Divisions 1967–68* (Hong Kong: Center of Contemporary Chinese Studies, 1969), p. 319.

34. *Current Scene 4,* no. 11 (July 1, 1968), p. 12.

35. *Important CCP Documents,* p. 315.

36. Institute of International Relations, *Chung-kung jen-ming-lu (Who's Who in Communist China),* op. cit., p. 738.

37. *Important CCP Documents,* p. 315.

38. Chien, op. cit., p. 291.

39. *Important CCP Documents,* p. 318.

40. Ibid.

41. *Chinese Communist Affairs Monthly 11,* no. 4 (June 1968), pp. 38–39.

42. "Document of the Chinese Communist Party Central Committee," *Current Background,* no. 852 (May 6, 1968), pp. 111–12.

43. Ibid., p. 112.

44. Ibid., pp. 111–12.

45. *Survey of China Mainland Press (Supp.),* no. 192 (July 17, 1967), pp. 7–15.

46. "Order of the Military Commission of the Chinese Communist Party Central Committee," *Current Background,* no. 852 (May 6, 1968), pp. 115–16.

47. *Wen Hui Pao* (Shanghai), April 28, 1967.

48. "Circular Order of the Chinese Communist Party Central Committee, the State Council, the Central Military Commission, and the Cultural Revolution Group Concerning the Strict Prohibition of Armed Struggle, Illegal Arrest, and Looting and Sabotage" (June 6, 1967), Union Research Institute, *CCP Documents of the Great Proletarian Cultural Revolution* (Hong Kong: Union Research Institute, 1968) (hereafter, *CCP Documents*), pp. 463–64.

49. Ibid.

50. *Red Flag,* no. 12 (1967); *Peking Review,* no. 32 (August 4, 1967), p. 39.

51. *Survey of China Mainland Press (Supp.),* no. 200 (March 8, 1968), p. 18, cited in Stanley Karnow, *Mao and China: From Revolution to Revolution* (New York: Viking Press, 1972), pp. 379–80.

52. "Lin Piao's Important Speech at a Conference of High Echelon Cadres of the PLA" (August 9, 1967), *1968 Yearbook,* p. 770.

53. *Survey of China Mainland Press,* no. 4002 (August 16, 1967), p. 3.

54. Hua-min Chung and Arthur C. Miller, *Madame Mao: A Profile of Chiang Ch'ing* (Hong Kong: Union Research Institute, 1968), p. 246.

55. Rice, op. cit., p. 357.

56. Asia Research Center, *The Great Power Struggle in China,* op. cit., p. 484.

57. Jurgen Domes, *The Internal Politics of China 1949-1972* (New York: Praeger, 1973), p. 189.

58. *The China Quarterly,* no. 33 (January/March 1968), p. 146.

59. Domes, op. cit., p. 191.

60. *Survey of China Mainland Press,* no. 4142 (March 20, 1968), p. 8.

61. *The China Quarterly,* no. 34 (April/June 1968), p. 175.

62. Ibid.

63. *CCP Documents,* p. 523.

64. Ibid., pp. 524-26.

65. Union Research Institute, *Communist China 1968* (Hong Kong: Union Research Institute, 1969), p. 24.

66. *Survey of China Mainland Press,* no. 4060 (November 15, 1967), pp. 1-2.

67. Chien, op. cit., p. 319.

68. "Speech by Chiang Ch'ing on September 5, 1967, When the Central Leaders Received Anhwei Representatives for the Third Time," *Survey of China Mainland Press (Supp.),* no. 209 (November 3, 1967), pp. 1-5.

69. "Premier Chou's Speech to the Representatives of the Mass Representatives of the Mass Organizations of the Canton Area," September 27, 1967, *Survey of China Mainland Press (Supp.),* no. 215 (January 19, 1968), pp. 1-12.

70. *Survey of China Mainland Press,* no. 4168 (May 1, 1968), p. 2.

71. "Order Issued by the Chinese Communist Party Central Committee, the State Council, the Central Military Affairs Committee, the Central Cultural Revolution Group Forbidding Seizure of Arms, Equipment and Other Military Supplies from the PLA" (September 5, 1967), *Survey of China Mainland Press,* no. 4026 (September 22, 1967), pp. 1-2.

72. *Survey of China Mainland Press,* no. 4190 (June 4, 1968), pp. 1-18.

73. Ibid.

74. "Important Speeches by Central Leaders on March 15, 1968," *Survey of China Mainland Press,* no. 4181 (May 20, 1968), p. 8; "Important Speeches by Central Leaders on March 18, 1968," *Survey of China Mainland Press,* no. 4182 (May 21, 1968), p. 6.

75. *Current Scene 6,* no. 21 (December 6, 1968), p. 17.

76. *Survey of China Mainland Press,* no. 4169 (May 2, 1968), pp. 4-5.

77. Ibid., p. 4.

78. *Studies on Chinese Communism 2,* no. 12 (1968), p. 117.

79. *Survey of China Mainland Press,* no. 4188 (May 29, 1968), p. 2, and no. 4186 (May, 1968), pp. 2-3.

80. *Studies on Chinese Communism 2,* no. 12 (1968), p. 117.

81. *Survey of China Mainland Press,* no. 4190 (June 5, 1968), pp. 1-18.

82. *Important CCP Documents,* p. 264.

83. "Chairman Mao's Latest Eighteen-Point Instructions," *Survey of China Mainland Press,* no. 4201 (June 19, 1968), p. 4.

84. Harvey Nelsen, "Military Forces in the Cultural Revolution," *The China Quarterly,* no. 51 (July/September 1972), pp. 461-62.

85. "Excerpts from Statements by Premier Chou En-lai and Other Central Leaders at Reception of Representatives from Kwangsi" (July 25, 1968), Chien, op. cit., p. 327.

86. Ibid., p. 328.

87. See *Summary of World Broadcasts* (London: British Broadcasting Corporation), p. 3, FE/2388, as quoted in *The China Quarterly,* no. 30 (April/June 1967), p. 222.

88. *People's Daily,* February 10, 1967.

89. *Red Flag,* no. 5 (1967); *Peking Review,* no. 12 (March 17, 1967), p. 16.

90. Ibid.

91. Ibid.

92. *Red Flag,* no. 4 (1967); *Peking Review,* no. 10 (March 3, 1967), p. 6.

93. *Red Flag,* no. 5 (1967); *Peking Review,* no. 12 (March 17, 1967), p. 15.

94. *Peking Review,* no. 12 (March 17, 1967), p. 16.

95. *People's Daily,* March 10, 1967.

96. *Peking Review,* no. 12 (March 17, 1967), p. 14.

97. The major sources of biographical information of the 29 Chairmen of the RCs are Union Research Institute, *Who's Who in Communist China* (Hong Kong: Union Research Institute, 1968), and Institute of International Relations, *Chung-kung Jen-ming-lu (Who's Who in Communist China)* (Taipei: Institute of International Relations, 1967).

98. Ibid.

99. *People's Daily,* March 10, 1967.

100. *Red Flag,* no. 5 (1967); *Peking Review,* no. 12 (March 17, 1967), p. 16.

101. *New China News Agency,* November 1, 1968.

102. *Survey of China Mainland Press,* no. 4334 (January 9, 1969), pp. 7–8.

103. Ibid., p. 9.

104. Ibid., p. 10.

105. Ibid., p. 6.

106. Ibid., p. 10.

107. Ibid.

108. Ibid.

109. The Constitution of the Communist Party of China, 1956, Article 16. Constitution.

110. Domes, op. cit., p. 205.

# 4

## REBUILDING THE CHINESE COMMUNIST PARTY AT THE NATIONAL LEVEL—THE NINTH PARTY CONGRESS

After repeated delays, the Ninth Party Congress was finally held, from April 1 to 24, 1969. That it had been long overdue was indicated by the fact that, as early as October 16, 1967, Hsieh Fu-chih, chairman of the Peking Municipal Revolutionary Committee, had said serious consideration was being given to holding the congress in May or June 1968, or, at least, having it concluded before National Day, October 1.[1] One month later, on November 27, 1967, the CC and the CCRG jointly issued a statement announcing:

The majority of our comrades suggested the convention of the Ninth Party Congress sometime before National Day of next year. ... Some recommended an earlier date—during the first half of the next year, if situations improve rapidly.[2]

In the 1968 New Year's joint editorial published by *People's Daily, Liberation Army Daily,* and *Red Flag,* "party rectification," to be accomplished through the convening of a new Party Congress, had been rated the most urgent of the five "fighting tasks." Yet months had slipped by, until October 1968, when the Twelfth Plenum of the Eighth CC took place instead. The plenum then had announced that the congress would be held at an "appropriate time."[3] Not until their next joint editorial, on New Year's Day, 1969, did the Chinese press accurately forecast that "the Ninth Party Congress will be convened this year."[4]

The Ninth Congress departed from previously established procedures for electing delegates to a national Party event of this magnitude, probably because of intensive bargaining among groups competing for political power and a desire on the part of the Maoists to insure prior approval of the issues under consideration before the congress met in official session. In 1956 the 1,026 regular and alternate delegates to the Eighth Party Congress had been elected by Party Congresses of "every province, autonomous region, [and] centrally-directed city and [of] Party organizations under the Central Committee, in the government and in the People's Liberation Army,"[5] which were convened five months before the Eighth Congress. However, the 1,512 delegates to the Ninth Party Congress, Peking claimed, were "unanimously chosen" in accordance with the decisions made at the Twelfth Plenum, which were never made public, and "through full democratic consultation by Party organizations at various levels and after seeking the opinions of the broad masses."[6]

In reality, because of the chaotic state of most Party organizations at the local level, only eight provinces out of the 29 administrative units were reported to have held Party Congresses.[7] In every instance, provincial RCs acted in place of the provincial Party congresses called for by the Party Constitution;[8] the diversity of their organization suggests the absence of any uniform or nationally regulated procedures, and attendance in most instances consisted primarily of PLA Party members. Of the eight provinces, only Hunan "discussed the list of those who represent the province at the Ninth National Party Congress."[9] Probably more indicative of what took place was the comment made by Hsieh Fu-chih that the Ninth Congress should be organized "from the top downward":

> The Congress should first be held by the Party Central Committee and then at the lower levels. In this way, it will be possible to insure that the rebels among Party members will be in the majority. The Party Central Committee may first compile a main list of candidates for the Party Congress and the provincial Party Committees. In this way, there can be guarantee. . . . To elect representatives first at the central level, then at the provincial level and then at the *hsien* level will result in a Party Central Committee of Chairman Mao with a programme of Mao Tse-tung's thought and his revolutionary line, which will insure the quality of the Party.[10]

Local participation, to the extent that it was taken into account in the election process, was heavily influenced by the military, who dominated the RCs and supported the election of delegates who shared their views, often to the exclusion of the leftists.[11] Thus, the leftists' input in the draft of the new constitution was offset by the military's control of provincial delegates.

Highly unusual was the degree of secrecy maintained throughout the proceedings of the Ninth Congress. No official announcement regarding the convention was made until 9:00 P.M. on April 1, following the completion of the opening session, which had begun at 5:00 P.M. Nothing more appeared in the mass media until the communique of April 14, and in all, only four communiques, Lin's "Political Report," and the Party Constitution were published; yet the Eighth Party Congress had printed over 715 pages of various speeches and documents.[12] None of the three "most important speeches" made by Mao at the opening session of the Ninth Congress, the plenary session on April 14, and the plenary session of the Ninth CC, was ever made known. Foreign guests were not invited to the Ninth Congress in contrast to the more open atmosphere prevailing at the Eighth Congress. For the Eighth, 56 invitations were sent to Communist and "friendly" parties, and at least 47 foreign delegations came and delivered congratulatory speeches subsequently published in the *People's Daily.*[13]

In addition, the 1969 Party Constitution, "unanimously" adopted on April 14, was not only brief (12 short articles as opposed to 60 lengthy ones in the 1956 Constitution), but also exceedingly vague when compared with the minutely detailed and carefully worded previous constitution. Among the several plausible explanations for the change, the most likely seems to have been the need to formulate controversial issues in such a fashion as to arouse no opposition or, if that proved impossible, to ignore them altogether.

Finally, the Congress took a protracted nine days to elect a new CC totaling 279 members (170 regular and 109 alternate members), which represented a 44 percent increase over the Eighth CC's membership of 170 (97 regular and 73 alternate members). This unexplained expansion could be the result of attempts to accommodate competing factions. Also unusual was the manner in which the names of the Ninth CC members were listed: by the number of strokes in their surnames—an arrangement roughly equivalent to the alphabetic order of Western language—rather than by the number of votes received, as was the practice of the Eighth CC, with the exception of Mao and Lin who appeared first and second, respectively. In addition to signifying the unique status of Mao and Lin, the new way of listing names most likely reflected the difficulty in deciding the relative ranking of the other members.

## THE AGENDA OF THE NINTH CONGRESS

The agenda of the Congress was announced in the April 1 communique: the "Political Report" by Lin Piao; the revision of the Party Constitution; and the election of the new Ninth CC.

### Lin Piao's "Political Report"

Lin Piao's "Political Report" could have been controversial; delivered on April 1 and adopted on April 14, it was discussed by the Congress "sentence by sentence." Moreover, the Congress sent both Lin's report and the revised constitution to the Secretariat of the Presidium for "modifications in wording," and the report was not made public until April 27. Nothing more than a recitation of Mao's Cultural Revolution line without any new or original contribution, the report was an extremely tedious opus of more than 24,000 words dealing with the domestic and foreign affairs of China.

Declaring that while a "great victory has been won," Lin candidly admitted in his account of the Cultural Revolution that there had been "twists and reversals,"[14] citing Liuist counterattacks from "the winter of 1966 to the spring of 1967"[15] and "fierce struggles" until September 1968, when RCs had been created in every province, autonomous region, and centrally directed city. Nevertheless, Lin asserted, that victory had been made possible by "relying on the wise leadership of Chairman Mao."[16] Echoing Mao, Lin continued, "The revolution is not yet over," and it would still be necessary to continue the "socialist revolution" to "carry out the tasks of struggle-criticism-transformation conscientiously,"[17] and urged "the living study and application of Mao Tse-tung Thought . . . [to] truly turn the whole country into a great school of Mao Tse-tung Thought,"[18] and attempted to intimidate any remaining Liuist sympathizers with the threat of punishment "by the whole Party and the whole nation."[19]

## The Revised Party Constitution

A draft constitution had been proposed by Mao in November 1967 and prepared by a ten-man commission including leading leftists as earlier mentioned. Though reflecting the philosophy and aims of the Cultural Revolution, it had been, nevertheless, written in a spirit of compromise calculated to insure its acceptance by, among others, the regional military leaders who were given considerable flexibility in determining the timing and election procedure of Party Congress delegates. After soliciting comments and suggestions from all RCs and Party organizations in the PLA, the Twelfth Plenum of the Eighth CC had subsequently approved the draft in October 1968.[20]

The constitution adopted by the Ninth Congress was essentially the same as the draft except for certain changes affecting the PLA. First, the new constitution included the PLA among those organizations which "must all accept the leadership of the Party."[21] Second, the Party attempted to tighten its control over the political activities of the PLA by making the decisions regarding the convening of Party congresses and the selection of Party committee members subject to the approval of higher Party organizations. Finally, the statement that primary Party organs must "persevere in the four firsts, and foster the three-eight working style in a big way," a slogan coined by Lin for the military, was dropped, as was a section that called upon the Party to learn from the political work style of the PLA. Overall, it appears that the Party intended to reassert its authority and persist in implementing the doctrine of "politics in command." Most likely Lin Piao was pressured into compromising on these issues, and hard bargaining was probably the reason for delayed publication of the constitution, in *People's Daily* on April 29, despite the fact that it was adopted "unanimously" on April 14.

## The Election of the Ninth Central Committee

The Party Congress elected a new CC—the Ninth—with a total membership of 279. A high political mortality rate, unprecedented in the history of the CCP, characterized the fate of members both of the Eighth CC and its Politburo. Of the 193 members of the Eighth CC,* 116 were now eliminated and 24 had died.[22] Those reelected, having apparently passed the loyalty test, numbered only 54, a mere 30 percent.[23] The Eighth Politburo had originally been composed of 17 full and 6 alternate members in 1956 with 3 alternates[24] added after its second session in 1958. Of these 26, only 9 survived to serve in the Ninth Politburo (Mao, Lin, Chou En-lai, Chu Teh, Tung Pi-wu, Liu Po-ch'eng, Li Hsien-nien, Ch'en Po-ta and K'ang Sheng); 11 were purged (Liu Shao-ch'i, Teng Hsiao-p'ing, P'eng Chen, P'eng Teh-huai, Ho Lung, Li Ching-ch'uan, T'an Chen-lin, Ulanfu, Chang Wen-t'ien, Lu Ting-yi, and Po I-po); 3 were demoted to only CC member status (Ch'en Yun, Ch'en Yi, and Li Fu-ch'un), and 3 died (Lin Po-chu, K'o Ch'ing-shih, and Lo Jung-huan).

## MAO'S RESURGENCE

For Mao, the Ninth Party Congress constituted a hard-fought victory over the Party machine loyal to Liu Shao-ch'i and Teng Hsiao-p'ing. At the congress, Lin in his "Political Report" officially condemned Liu Shao-ch'i as "the arch representative of the persons in power taking the capitalist road,"[25] and expelled him from the Party for the second time. Teng, spared formal denunciation, was quietly dropped from the Ninth CC, and other prominent anti-Maoists faded into obscurity or simply disappeared. To prevent their possible return, the new Party Constitution stipulated:

> Proven renegades, enemy agents, absolutely unrepentant persons in power taking the capitalist road, degenerates and alien class elements must be cleared out of the Party and not be re-admitted.[26]

---

*In 1958 at the Second Session of the Eighth Party Congress, two alternate members, Yang Hsien-chen and Wang En-mao, were "promoted" to regular status to fill the vacancies resulting from the deaths of Huang Ching and Lan Jo-yu. At the same time, 25 additional alternate members were "elected."

As a precaution against any future recruits with bourgeois backgrounds, Party membership was limited to any "Chinese worker, poor peasant, lower-middle peasant, revolutionary army man or any other revolutionary element,"[27] while the 1956 Constitution had allowed any Chinese to apply "who works and does not exploit the labor of others."[28]

In a complete reversal of the 1956 provision, the 1969 Party Constitution reaffirmed the importance of Mao's Thought by asserting that "the Communist Party of China takes Marxism-Leninism-Mao Tse-tung Thought as the theoretical basis guiding its thinking,"[29] and proclaimed that Mao "integrated the universal truth of Marxism-Leninism with the concrete practice of revolution, inherited, defended and developed Marxism-Leninism and has brought it to a higher and completely new stage."[30]

## LIN PIAO AS MAO'S OFFICIAL SUCCESSOR

In a move without precedence in the history of the international Communist movement, the 1969 Party constitution officially designated Lin Piao as Mao's successor. Described as Mao's "closest comrade in arms," Lin was praised for having "consistently held high the great red banner of Mao Tse-tung Thought and . . . most loyally and resolutely carried out and defended Comrade Mao Tse-tung's proletarian revolutionary line."[31]

As Lin, then, rose to the number two position in the Party, many of his supporters rode his coattails, becoming CC members for the first time. Specifically, there were, among the 19 full mumbers of the Politburo of the CC (excluding Mao and Lin) 5 of Lin's supporters (Yeh Ch'un, Li Tso-p'eng, Wu Fa-hsien, Ch'iu Hui-tso, and Huang Yung-sheng) who had never before sat in the CC.

## MILITARY DOMINANCE

The dominant role played by the PLA in the Cultural Revolution, coupled with the rise of Lin, resulted in a sharp increase in military representation in all bodies of the Ninth Party Congress and especially in the CC. Delegates to the Congress elected a 176-man Presidium, with Mao as its chairman, Lin Piao, its vice-chairman, and Chou En-lai, its secretary general. In the Presidium, military representation amounted to over 35 percent of its total.[32] Besides the 32 chairmen and vice-chairmen of the 29 RCs, an additional 51 were elected who could also be classified as military leaders. From the 13 MRs came 9 commanders and 9 political commissars, and 7 commanders and 8 political commissars came from the MDs.[33] The remaining members, divided equally between the cadres and representatives of the masses, totaled less than 100 delegates.

The percentage of military representation in the Ninth CC also increased. Of the 279 members, 132, or approximately 45 percent, were military commanders or political commissars. Seventy-seven, or 27 percent, were cadres, and 56, or 20 percent, the so-called revolutionary rebels.[34]

In the Ninth Politburo, military predominance was equally conspicuous. Excluding Mao, 13 of the members were military men,[35] in sharp contrast to the 7 of 27 members in the Eighth Politburo who could be so described. It is also noteworthy that 10 of these 13 military men were new to national prominence. The other 11 members were leading Party cadres and government officials,[36] including two women, Chiang Ch'ing and Yeh Ch'ün, who both, incidentally, wore PLA uniforms to the Congress. Their election to the Politburo for the first time clearly indicated the influence and prominence of their husbands, Mao and Lin respectively.

## THE EMERGENCE OF MASS REPRESENTATIVES

Besides ridding himself of his opponents, Mao succeeded in reorganizing the Party hierarchy to reflect the changed balance of power and, in doing so, acknowledged the existence of a new political force, the mass representatives. Approximately 20 percent, or "one-quarter,"[37] of the Ninth CC membership came from this category, now admitted for the first time as a group to the inner sanctums of Party power. Unlike members of the old Party elite who rose to prominence via the established paths, the majority of mass representatives gained recognition and acquired Party favor by virtue of their energetic efforts in the radical cause during the Cultural Revolution. To facilitate their admission to the Party, the new Party Constitution even eliminated the one-year probationary period for new members as prescribed earlier.[38]

## ATTEMPTS AT CENTRALIZATION

The 1956 Party Constitution had attempted to correct improper and excessive centralism,[39] which had paid only perfunctory attention to local problems and conditions and needlessly compounded many of the problems encountered by basic-level Party organizations in their work. To demarcate the jurisdictional perimeters of Party committees at different levels, the 1956 Party Constitution had specifically provided:

All questions of a national character or questions that require a uniform decision for the whole country shall be handled by the central Party organizations, so as to contribute to the centralism and unity of the Party. All questions of a local character or questions that need to be decided locally shall be handled by the local Party organizations, so as to find solutions appropriate to the local conditions. The functions and powers of higher local Party organizations and those of lower local Party organizations shall be appropriately divided according to the same principle.[40]

The 1969 Party Constitution blurred these distinctions by not defining the functions and powers of Party organizations at different levels and recommending only a "simple and efficient structure" under "unified leadership."[41] No provision was made for the Party secretariat, the previous stronghold of Teng Hsiao-p'ing, which, according to the 1956 Constitution, "should attend to the daily work of the Central Committee under the direction of the Politburo and its Standing Committee."[42] Instead the 1969 Constitution provided for the establishment of "a number of necessary organs . . . to attend to the day-to-day work of the Party, the government and the army in a centralized way."[43] Furthermore, Party members were no longer obligated to "carry out unconditionally" decisions with which they disagreed and, in direct contradiction to Teng's earlier recommendations of decentralization, were allowed "to bypass the immediate leadership and report directly to higher levels"[44]—the CC and even its chairman.

The representation of provincial-level leaders, Party as well as military, rose sharply in the Ninth CC, reversing the previous ratio of two to one in favor of national leaders working from Peking.[45] More than 50 percent of the CC members with a military background came from MDs and MRs, and the percentage of locally based cadres was almost as high.[46] Indeed, a strong local power base seems to have provided the most expedient way to high office in the national Party hierarchy as well as the local bureaucracy.


## CHOU EN-LAI OVERSHADOWED

Probably because of his moderate and pragmatic positions, Chou suffered a temporary setback. This is most clearly illustrated by his changing position in the Standing Committee of both the Eighth and Ninth CCs.

In 1956, the Standing Committee had been composed of the chairman, Mao Tse-tung, and four vice-chairmen, Liu Shao-ch'i, Chou En-lai, Chu Teh, and Ch'en Yün, with two additional members added in 1958: Lin Piao, the new fifth vice-chairman, and Teng Hsiao-p'ing, secretary general of the Party secretariat. The Eleventh Plenum of the Eighth CC reportedly enlarged the Standing Committee to 11 members.[47] Then in the Ninth CC the Standing Committee was whittled down to five: Mao, Lin Piao, Ch'en Po-ta, Chou En-lai, and K'ang Sheng. In the official list, Mao and Lin appeared first and second, but the other three were again listed according to the number of strokes in their surnames instead of their relative standing in the Party hierarchy. Thus, Chou En-lai, who has always occupied the third position, was now in fourth place below Ch'en Po-ta.

The Ninth Party Congress represented a coalition between the Maoists and the Lin Piao faction at the national level. They succeeded in eliminating their opposition and were able to strike a balance through mutual accommodation at the expense of Chou En-lai, who apparently lost some of his former stature and found himself playing "fourth fiddle." Yet the overall situation in China remained extremely volatile. For one thing, Ch'en Po-ta faded from the scene in 1970. The joint editorial (*People's Daily, Liberation Army Daily,* and *Red Flag*) on July 1 commemorating the fiftieth anniversary of the CCP ominously noted that the "humble little commoner" was "actually a big careerist,"[48] a reference to a speech Ch'en had given at Peita in 1966 in which he called himself a "humble little commoner," feigning a willingness to learn from the masses.[49] *People's Daily* mentioned Ch'en for the last time on August 2, 1970; subsequently, he vanished without a trace. Further, the dominance of the military at the provincial and local levels was short-lived. Though able to obtain a large percentage of leadership positions in the PPCs at the time of their creation, the military gradually lost ground in the ensuing years as the Party reasserted its authority and control.

## NOTES

1. *Survey of China Mainland Press,* no. 4097 (January 11, 1968), p. 2.

2. Institute for the Study of Chinese Communist Problems, *1968 Yearbook on Chinese Communism* (Taipei: Institute for the Study of Chinese Communist Problems, 1968) (hereafter, *1968 Yearbook*), p. 580. See also Union Research Institute, *Communist China 1967* (Hong Kong: Union Research Institute, 1969), pp. 179–84.

3. *People's Daily,* November 2, 1968. *Peking Review,* no. 45 (November 8, 1968), p. 3.

4. *People's Daily,* January 1, 1969.

5. *People's Daily,* September 15, 1956. The only exception was Tibet, where the Party Congress was held in January instead of May.

6. *Peking Review,* no. 18 (April 30, 1969), p. 41.

7. These were Chekiang, Kweichow, Hunan, Hupei, Honan, Kwangtung, Szechwan, and Yunnan. See *China News Analysis,* no. 746 (February 28, 1969), pp. 3–5.

8. Ralph L. Powell, "The Party, the Government and the Gun," *Asian Survey 10,* June 1970, p. 452.

9. *China News Analysis,* no. 746 (February 28, 1969), p. 3.

10. *Survey of China Mainland Press,* no. 4097 (January 1, 1968), p. 2.

11. Stanley Karnow, *Mao and China: From Revolution to Revolution* (New York: Viking Press, 1972), p. 452.

12. Gordon A. Bennett, "China's Continuing Revolution: Will It Be Permanent?," *Asian Survey,* January 1970, p. 9.

13. *People's Daily,* September 22, 1956, still maintained that "fifty-five delegations from the communist or labor parties of other countries had arrived as of September 18, except that from Japan because of preventive action taken by the Japanese Government."

14. *Peking Review,* no. 18 (April 30, 1969), p. 23.

15. Ibid., p. 22.

16. Ibid., p. 23.

17. Ibid., p. 24.

18. Ibid.

19. Ibid., p. 29.

20. For the draft proposal, see *The China Quarterly,* no. 37 (January/March, 1969), pp. 169–73.

21. *Peking Review,* no. 18 (April 30, 1969), p. 38.

22. *Central Daily News,* (Taipei), May 4, 1969.

23. Bennett, op. cit., p. 4.

24. *The China Quarterly,* no. 39 (July/September 1969), p. 146.

25. Lin Piao, op. cit., p. 18, 21.

26. "The Constitution of the Communist Party of China, 1969," Article 4 (hereafter 1969 Party Constitution) in *Peking Review,* no. 18 (April 30, 1969), pp. 36–39.

27. 1969 Party Constitution, Article 1.

28. "The Constitution of the Communist Party of China, 1956," Article 1 (hereafter, 1956 Party Constitution), in Peter H. Tang, *Communist China Today (Vol. II): Chronological and Documentary Supplement* (New York: Praeger, 1958), pp. 112–33.

29. 1969 Party Constitution, General Program.

30. Ibid.

31. Ibid.

32. See John Gittings, "A Cool Congress," *Far Eastern Economic Review,* no. 15 (April 10, 1969), p. 78.

33. *Central Daily News,* April 6, 1969.

34. *1968 Yearbook,* p. 581.

35. See *China News Analysis,* no. 758 (May 23, 1969), pp. 3–4.

36. Ibid., pp. 5–6.

37. A. Doak Barnett, *Uncertain Passage* (Washington, D.C.: Brookings, 1974), p. 233.

38. Compare Article 4, 1956 Party Constitution, with Article 2, 1969 Party Constitution.

39. *Chinese Communist Affairs Monthly 12,* no. 5 (July 1969), p. 54.

40. 1956 Party Constitution, Article 25.

41. 1969 Party Constitution, Article 7.

42. 1956 Party Constitution, Article 37.

43. 1969 Party Constitution, Article 9.

44. Ibid., Article 4.

45. Donald W. Klein and Lois B. Hager, "The Ninth Central Committee," *The China Quarterly,* no. 45 (January/March 1971), p. 41.

46. *Elites in the People's Republic of China,* ed. Robert A. Scalapino (Seattle: University of Washington Press, 1972), p. 143.

47. See "CCP Order of Precedence," *The China Quarterly,* no. 28 (October/December 1966), pp. 186–87.

48. *Peking Review,* no. 27 (July 2, 1971), p. 20.

49. Jack Chen, *Inside the Cultural Revolution* (New York: Macmillan, 1975), p. 326. It was clear that the "humble little commoner" referred to Ch'en since Chiang Ch'ing had also called him by the same name in her April 12, 1967, speech: "Comrade Po-ta always says that he is a 'humble little commoner.' I then am even smaller." See *Chinese News Analysis,* no. 851 (August 13, 1971), p. 2, or Institute for the Study of Chinese Communist Problems, *Important CCP Documents of the Great Proletarian Cultural Revolution* (Taipei: Institute for the Study of Chinese Communist Problems, 1973), p. 303.

# 5

## NEW FACTIONAL COALITIONS IN THE CHINESE COMMUNIST PARTY AT THE PROVINCIAL LEVEL

The RCs had been created as part of an extensive campaign to stem widespread disorder and violence, and were specifically intended to be no more than temporary organs of power. Once normalcy had returned to the provinces, the provincial Party organizations had to be revitalized so that they could again serve as a vital link between the provinces and the central authorities.

The first PPC to be reestablished was the one in Hunan, on December 13, 1970,[1] and other provinces soon followed suit. By August 26, 1971, the process of rebuilding the CCP at the provincial level had been completed when Heilungkiang announced the formation of the twenty-ninth PPC.[2]

## PROVINCIAL PARTY CONGRESSES

The PPCs were elected by provincial party congresses in a way similar to the election of the CC by the National Party Congress. The duration, size, and delegate composition of these congresses differed from province to province. They met for periods of three to ten days and varied in size independent of provincial population. There was apparently no standardized procedure for delegate selections; in fact the reports in the *New China News Agency* showed unusual variance in this matter. In some provinces (such as Kiangsu, Honan, Kirin, Kweichow, Shantung, Shansi, and Inner Mongolia) there was no proclaimed policy outlined, or only vague statements that delegates came from "various fronts of the province."[3] In others, scattered evidence seemed to indicate that, in the absence of a policy promulgated by central authorities, each province probably established election criteria on the basis of local exigencies. In Hunan, for example, delegates came from party members among the industrial workers and poor and lower-middle peasants, those in the People's Liberation Army units stationed in Hunan, and those among revolutionary leading cadres, Red Guards, revolutionary intellectuals and people of minority nationalities. Women delegates made up a certain portion.[4]

In other provinces representation was less inclusive. In Shanghai, a unique case, it was biased toward Party members among workers (51 percent) and women (26 percent).[5] Among provinces with substantial minority population, the Ch'inghai delegation also included, for example, Tibetan, Hui, Mongolian, Tu, Sala, and Kazakh nationalities[6] in addition to Han Chinese; the Kwangsi delegation included Chuang, Yao, Miao, Tung, and "six other nationalities."[7]

Official sources described the election procedure for provincial delegates as being similar to that of the National Party Congress—"through full democratic consultation by the Party organizations at various levels and after taking note of the views from the broad masses outside the Party."[8] Non-Party organizations were consulted as a result of the renewed emphasis on the "mass line." In the election of delegates to the Shanghai Municipal Party Congress, for example, organizations such as the Workers' Association, the Peasants' Association, and the Association of Activists in Studying Mao Tse-tung's Thought reportedly took part. There is little evidence, however, to suggest that these participants played a decisive part.

The provincial party congresses "elected" members of the PPCs "according to the provision of the new Party Constitution and through full democratic consultation"[9] even though no such election procedure was elaborated in the new constitution. Nor was it clear how the process of "full democratic consultation" was implemented or to what extent procedures followed the pattern of those of the Ninth Party Congress, which were described in similar terms.[10] In any event, the election resulted in the creation of PPCs that differed significantly from their earlier counterparts.

The new PPCs were larger than their predecessors. Before the Cultural Revolution, the PPCs generally averaged about 30 or 40 members. When they were formed, they ranged in size from 45 members in Chinghai to 106 in Szechwan, totaling 2,140 members. In addition, there were 572 alternate members, positions that did not exist in the old PPCs. There was a similar increase in the membership of the standing committees of the PPCs which "exercise all the powers of the full committee" and "actually run day-to-day Party affairs."[11] The total membership of the standing committees was at least 405; the smallest, the Kiangsu PPC, consisted of 9 members, and the largest, the Szechwan PPC, had 19. Thus the total number of PPC members, including standing committee members, has increased but the gain varied from province to province and bore no direct relationship to provincial population.

Within the PPCs, the executive secretariat consisted of four positions: first secretary (*ti-i shu-chi*), second secretary (*ti-erh-shu-chi*), secretary (*shu-chi*), and deputy secretary (*fu-shu-chi*). The secretariat is elected by the PPC but subject to the approval of the CC. As before, every PPC was headed by a first secretary, generally regarded as the most powerful man in the province. A. Doak Barnett's observation about the *hsien* first secretary is equally applicable to the PPC first secretary:

> His opinions carried more weight than those of any other individual, and he was responsible for directing the entire range of work carried out by both Party and government organs.[12]

In addition to first secretaries, 14 PPCs had second secretaries.* Apparently, this position was established to provide assistance for first secretaries who have multiple duties (such as those commanding an MR as well as chairing an RC in that region), or who hold important positions in Peking necessitating prolonged absences from the province. The first secretaries of MPCs of all three centrally directed cities (Peking, Shanghai, and Tientsin) had second secretaries to assist them with the complex job of managing urban centers. A second secretary also was installed in every PPC where a revolutionary cadre was the first secretary and, in all cases except Shanghai, he was a military figure who might be expected to monitor, if not supervise, Party operations. Other known members of the PPC secretariats included 84 secretaries and 31 deputy secretaries.

The extensive reorganization of the Party which resulted from the Cultural Revolution was reflected in the purge of the old PPC secretaries. Of the 29 first secretaries who held office before 1966, only 3 survived the tumult unscathed and retained their original posts, while 4 were demoted to secretary.† Only 29 of 253 pre-Cultural Revolution section secretaries and secretar-

---

*The following PPCs have second secretaries: Chinghai, Fukien, Heilungkiang, Hopei, Hupei, Liaoning, Ninghsia, Shantung, Sinkiang, Szechwan, Yunnan, Peking, Shanghai, and Tientsin.

†Retaining their posts were Liu Chien-hsun (Honan PPC), Liu Tzu-hou (Hopei PPC), and Wei Kuo-ch'ing (Kwangsi Chuang ARPC). Of the four demoted, T'an Ch'i-lung, originally the first secretary of the Shantung PPC, was reassigned to the Fukien PPC as one of the five secretaries; Chang P'ing-hua, once the first secretary of Hunan, was "liberated" and reappointed as a secretary of Shansi PPC; Chao Tzu-yang, the previous first secretary of Kwangtung PPC, became a secretary of the Inner Mongolia ARPC; and Chang T'i-hsueh, first secretary of Hupei PPC, whose demotion did not involve a transfer outside the province, became one of five secretaries of the same committee.

ies remained in the present PPCs: 8 were promoted, 10 continued to serve as secretary, and 11 were demoted to deputy secretary.*

## PROVINCIAL PARTY SECRETARIES

In most instances, biographical information is available only on the first secretaries.[13] Data concerning the other secretaries are fragmentary, and reliable generalization is difficult. Nevertheless, a basic profile of this provincial elite can be sketched by examining such characteristics as their age, sex, minority status, professional background, and membership on the CC and provincial RCs.

### Age

Like most of the members of the CC, the majority of the first secretaries were old Party faithfuls. Of 29 first secretaries, the ages of 20 (69 percent) were known. At the time the PPCs were created, the youngest, Ch'eng Shih-ch'ing (Kiangsi PPC) was 54, while the oldest, Hsieh Fu-chih (Peking MPC) was 75 when he died on March 26, 1972; their average age being 62. Further, of the 14 second secretaries, the average age of the 8 (57 percent) whose age was known was 58, indicating that most of the second secretaries probably belonged to the same generation as the first secretaries; Yao Wen-yuan (Shanghai MPC) was the youngest at 37, while Liang Hsing-ch'u (Szechwan PPC), who was in his early sixties, was probably the oldest. The ages of 34 (40 percent) of the 84 secretaries were known; the youngest were Wang Hung-wen and Wang Hsiu-chen, both secretaries of the Shanghai MPC and born around 1941. Ch'en Yu (Kwangtung PPC), reportedly born in 1892, was probably the oldest secretary. The average of the 34 ages known was 56; only 3 were in their

---

*According to available information, 8 secretaries were promoted: Chang Ch'un-ch'iao (Shanghai MPC); Chou Hsing (Yunnan PPC); Chou Ch'ih-p'ing (Fukien PPC); Saifudin (Sinkiang ARPC); Chiang Yi (Hupei PPC); Yu Chieh (Heilungkiang PPC); Cheng Chi-chiao (Kirin PPC); and Chia T'ing-san (Kweichow PPC). The ten secretaries who retained their original posts were Chang Lin-ch'ih (Heilungkiang PPC); Chi Teng-k'uei (Honan PPC); Ch'en Yu (Kwangtung PPC); Ma Tien-shui (Shanghai MPC); Hu Chi-tsung (Kansu PPC); Juan Po-sheng (Kirin PPC); Yang Tung-sheng (Tibet ARPC); Wu Te and Ting Kuo-yu (Peking MPC); and Li Ta-chang (Szechwan PPC). And, as far as can be determined, the eleven demoted secretaries were: Pai Tung-ts'ai (Kiangsi PPC); P'eng Ch'ung (Kiangsu PPC); Yang Ch'un-fu (Liaoning PPC); Lai K'o-k'o (Chekiang PPC); An P'ing-sheng (Kwangsi PPC); Hsiao Ch'un (Shensi PPC); Hsueh Hung-fu (Chinghai PPC); Li Li (Kweichow PPC); Ma Li (Hopei PPC); Pai Ju-ping and Su Yi-jan (Shantung PPC).

thirties and 2 in their forties.* Of the 31 deputy secretaries, only the age of Lü Yü-lan (Hopei PPC) was known: she was 32 at the time. The deputy secretaries were probably younger than the other secretaries; their low status and comparative obscurity being attributable in part to their youth.

Party cadres of the younger generation were not well represented in the PPCs. Their absence was especially characteristic of the higher ranks, despite the Party's pronouncements that it was "getting rid of the stale and taking in the fresh"[14] and the fact that its claim that "the new Provincial Party Committee is a 'three-in-one' combination of old, middle-aged and young people"[15] was basically not met.

## Sex

It is noteworthy that not one first secretary was a female, although there was token representation of women in other ranks. Three secretaries (Wang Hsiu-chen, Wang Man-t'ien, and Pa Sang) and three deputy secretaries (Lu Yu-lan, Wu Kuei-hsien, and Chao Chin-ch'iang) were women. Unlike some of their counterparts in the CC, whose election may be ascribed to the stature and influence of their husbands, these female secretaries acquired their positions on their own merits. Two (Lü Yü-lan and Pa Sang) have been described as representatives of poor and lower-middle peasants, while another two (Wang Hsiu-chen and Wu Kuei-hsien) were regarded as model workers. Furthermore, two were members of the CC (Wang Hsiu-chien and Lü Yü-lan) and all six occupy positions of vice-chairman or member in the RC of their respective provinces.

## Minority Status

Originally, there were 9 members of the PPC secretariats who belonged to national minorities. Wei Kuo-ch'ing, of the Kwangsi Chuang Autonomous Region Party Committee (ARPC), was the only minority first secretary. He had been "a trusted comrade," associated with the Chinese Communist movement since the 1930s. Also a Long March veteran and a major-general in the army, he has served in many important posts, primarily but not exclusively in his native province of Kwangsi. Saifudin, of Sinkiang ARPC, and Uighur, was the only minority second secretary. He has been promoted from his original position as secretary, which he occupied from 1956 to 1965.

---

*Wang Hung-wen, Wang Hsiu-chen, and P Sang, born in 1940, were the three secretaries in their thirties; Pu Chan-ya (Hunan PPC) and Chi Teng-k'uei (Honan PPC), in their forties.

Unlike its pre-Cultural Revolution predecessor, which was dominated by Han cadres, the secretariat of the Tibet ARPC had 3 Tibetan secretaries (T'ien Pao, Yang Tung-sheng, and Pa Sang) out of a total of 6. Another Tibetan, Talo, served as a deputy secretary in the Chinghai PPC. Two deputy secretaries of the Ninghsia ARPC, Wang Chih-ch'iang and Chao Chih-ch'iang, are Hui. In the Inner Mongolian ARPC, which has 4 secretaries, Wu T'ao was the only Mongol. This is a dramatic departure from the past when "the Mongol domination of the secretariat [was] virtually complete."[16]

All minority secretaries except Talo served in their native region. Thus, like minority officials in the Soviet Union, the careers of Chinese minority cadres seem to confirm the observation that they are "limited to minority areas."[17] Besides giving credence to the Party's claim of equal treatment of all nationalities, the use of minority cadres in their home towns is obviously intended to assure effective liaison between the PPC and the local population. Nationality, therefore, still seemed to be one of the crucial criteria in deciding cadre assignment by the Party.

## Central Committee Membership

As might be expected, the overwhelming majority of the first secretaries, 27 (93.1 percent), were on the Ninth CC; 23 were regular members, including 5 who were also members of the powerful 21-man Politburo (Hsieh Fu-chih, Chang Ch'un-ch'iao, Li Teh-sheng, Hsu Shih-yu, and Ch'en Hsi-lien), and 4 were alternate members (Wang Chia-tao, Yu T'ai-chung, Lan Yi-nung, and K'ang Chien-min). The only 2 first secretaries who failed to gain CC membership were Hsieh Chen-hua of the Shansi PPC and Jen Jung of the Tibet ARPC.* Of the 14 second secretaries, 11 (78.6 percent) were members of the CC. These include Cheng San-sheng (Hopei PPC) and Chang Chiang-lin (Ch'inghai PPC), who were alternate members, and Yao Wen-yuan, who was also a Politburo member. Thirty-two (38 percent) of 84 secretaries were members of the CC, 12 serving as alternates. The percentage of those holding membership on the CC declined sharply at the deputy secretary level. Of the 31 deputy secretaries, only 7 (22.6 percent) were members of the CC, including 4 alternates.

---

*Both are relative newcomers to political prominence. Hsieh, an obscure soldier, was a dark horse whose quick ascendency to power surprised many seasoned observers of the China scene. Jen, a deputy political commissar of the Tibet MD for several years, was installed by the central authorities to eradicate the remnant influence of Chang Kuo-hua, who ruled Tibet as an "independent kingdom" before and during the Cultural Revolution.

## Revolutionary Committee Membership

The relationship between the personnel of the PPCs and the RCs was very close: 28 (96.5 percent) of the 29 first secretaries in the PPCs also held important positions in the RCs of their respective provinces.* Of the 28, 22 were RC chairmen, 1 was an acting chairman, and 5 were vice-chairmen. The only exception is Yu T'ai-chung of the Inner Mongolia ARPC, who had held important military positions in Kiangsu and Peking before replacing T'eng Hui-ch'ing, the chairman of the Inner Mongolian RC, who had disappeared around October 1969. Of the 14 PPC second secretaries, 9 (64.3 percent) served as RC vice-chairmen, while the remaining 5 had no official positions. Further, 67 (79.7 percent) of the 84 PPC secretaries have held concurrent posts in their respective RCs; 60 were vice-chairmen and 7 were standing committee members. And 25 (80.6 percent) of the 31 PPC deputy secretaries also held concurrent positions in their respective RCs; 23 were vice-chairmen and 2 were Standing Committee members. The pre-Cultural Revolution practice of "intertwined but not identical Party and governmental hierarchies"[18] has been more than just restored; now the overlap between the two has become far greater.[19] "Liberation" of Party cadres serving in the PPCs prior to the Cultural Revolution was notably accelerated. At the time of the formation of the PPCs they constituted 75 percent compared with 60 percent in the RCs.[20] In almost every instance, they strengthened the PPCs in terms of experience and administrative capability.[21]

## THE NEW COALITION

Like the RCs, the PPCs were organized in accordance with the "three-in-one combination." However, the ascendency of the military to a dominant role was even more conspicuous in the composition of the PPCs. As shown in Table 2, the military occupied 60 percent of all positions in the PPC secretariats in 1971. This figure increased strikingly in the higher echelons: 76 percent of the first secretaries and 79 percent of the second secretaries had military backgrounds. By contrast, professional cadres were relegated to second-class status. Only 7 held first secretary posts, and in each of these cases, a member of the PLA was assigned as second secretary. The Shanghai MPC was the only committee with a civilian majority (3 cadres, 3 mass representa-

---

*Yu T'ai-chung was the only first secretary with no official position on the RC. He was, however, the former chairman of Wusih Municipal RC in Kiangsu province. ·

tives, and 1 military figure). The percentage of professional cadres among secretaries increased slightly at the lower ranks, but only at the lowest level of deputy secretary did they constitute a bare majority, of 52 percent.

Representation of mass organizations in the PPC secretariats was minimal, and all such representation was concentrated in the lower ranks: 6 were secretaries and 3 were deputy secretaries. The "triple alliance," as implemented, did not substantiate the original proclamation that "all three groups are equally indispensable."[22] In comparison with the RCs, where mass representatives constituted 37.9 percent of the total membership, the role of the masses in the PPCs was definitely downgraded.

Many provincial Party secretaries not only came from the ranks of the military but, more importantly, continued to hold military positions concurrently with their Party posts; 7 first secretaries were commanders or deputy commanders of the 11 MRs, and another 7 were political commissars or deputy political commissars at this level.* Further, 4 were commanders of the

## TABLE 2

### Composition of the Provincial Party Committees in 1971

| | Position | | | | |
|---|---|---|---|---|---|
| | First Secretary | Second Secretary | Secretary | Deputy Secretary | Total |
| PLA | | | | | |
| Number | 22 | 11 | 49 | 12 | 94 |
| Percent | 75.8 | 78.6 | 58.3 | 38.7 | 59.5 |
| Cadres | | | | | |
| Number | 7 | 3 | 29 | 16 | 55 |
| Percent | 24.1 | 21.4 | 34.5 | 51.6 | 34.8 |
| Masses | | | | | |
| Number | 0 | 0 | 6 | 3 | 9 |
| Percent | 0 | 0 | 7.1 | 9.7 | 5.7 |
| TOTAL | 29 | 14 | 84 | 31 | 158 |

Source: Based on data from Chung-kung yen-chiu, Chung-kung nien-pao, and Fei-ch'ing yueh-pao.

*The seven first secretaries who are also commanders or deputy commanders were Han Hsien-ch'u (Foochow MR); Tseng Ssu-yu (Wuhan MR); Hsu Shih-yu (Nanking MR); Chen Hsi-lien (Mukden MR); K'ang Chien-min (Lanchow MR); Yang Teh-chih (Tsinan MR); and Lung Shu-chin (Sinkiang MR). The seven first secretaries who are also political commissars or deputy political commissars were Chang Ch'un-ch'iao (Shanghai Garrison); Hsieh Hsueh-kung (Tientsin Garrison); Liu Chien-hsun (Wuhan MR); Hsien Heng-han (Lanchow MR); Liu Hsing-yuan (Canton MR); Li Jui-shan (Lanchow MR); and Chang Kuo-hua (Chengtu MR).

24 MDs or troop units stationed there, while another 5 were political commissars.* Of the 14 second secretaries, 12 were commanders or political commissars or had the ambiguous title of "responsible person" at the MR or MD level; and at least 51 (61 percent) of the 84 secretaries and 10 (32 percent) of the 31 deputy secretaries also had military assignments.

Association with one of the five "Field Army Systems" described by William Whitson also seems to have been a significant factor in the careers of some of the new provincial elite.[23] Of the 22 first secretaries with military background, at least 7 can be identified as close associates of Lin Piao through their service in the Fourth Field Army or its predecessor, the 115th Division of the Eighth Route Army. Another 5 first secretaries were associated with the Second Field Army, which now had jurisdiction over Peking and Inner Mongolia, MRs normally under the control of the North China Field Army, earlier referred to as the "Fifth" Field Army.

The First Field Army has been widely regarded as the power base of P'eng Teh-huai and Ho Lung. P'eng was discredited in 1959,[24] and Ho was implicated in an attempted coup in 1966.[25] Since the Cultural Revolution, the First Field Army continued to be penalized. Only 2 first secretaries with military background can be identified with this army, and both were stationed in the Lanchow MR, the traditional territory of the First Field Army. There are only 2 first secretaries who had close affiliation with the Third Field Army (once headed by Ch'en Yi, who was severely criticized during the Cultural Revolution in spite of Chou En-lai's strenuous defense); surprisingly, neither was assigned to the Nanking or Foochow MR, areas which the Third Field Army usually controls.

Unquestionably, the most striking characteristic of the PPCs was their unprecedented dominance by the military. For all practical purposes, the PLA has replaced the Party hierarchy at the provincial level; and the rudimentary separation of powers among the Party, the military, the provincial people's congresses, and the people's councils, which existed prior to the Cultural Revolution, simply disappeared. The concentration of PLA power in interlocking directorates of governing organizations at different levels was without parallel. Few could have anticipated, however, that the issue of military dominance was to explode shortly, dragging down Lin Piao in its wake.

---

*The four commanders were Li Teh-sheng (Anhwei MD); Liu Hsien-ch'uan (Ch'inghai MD); Wang Chia-tao (Heilungkiang MD); and Hsieh Chen-hua (Shansi MD). The five political commissars are Nan P'ing (Chekiang MD); Wang Huai-hsiang (Kirin MD); Ch'eng Shih-ch'ing (Kiangsi MD); Wei Kuo-ch'ing (Kwangsi MD); and Jen Jung (Tibet MD).

# NOTES

1. *New China News Agency,* December 14, 1970.

2. *Survey of China Mainland Press,* no. 4969, September 7–10, 1971, pp. 35–38.

3. *New China News Agency,* January 30, 1970.

4. *Survey of China Mainland Press,* no. 4803 (December 21–24, 1970), p. 2.

5. *Current Background,* no. 939 (September 17, 1971), p. 10.

6. Ibid., p. 18.

7. *New China News Agency,* February 20, 1971.

8. Ibid., December 31, 1971.

9. Ibid.

10. For details, see the "Press Communique of the Secretariat of the Presidium of the Ninth National Congress of the Communist Party of China (April 24, 1969)" in *Peking Review,* no. 18 (April 30, 1969), p. 44.

11. A. Doak Barnett, *Cadres, Bureaucracy and Political Power in Communist China* (New York: Columbia University Press, 1967), pp. 127–28.

12. Ibid., pp. 134–35.

13. All biographical data are taken from Donald W. Klein and Anne B. Clark, *Biographical Dictionary of Chinese Communism: 1921–1965* (Cambridge: Harvard University Press, 1971); Union Research Institute, *Who's Who in Communist China* (Hong Kong: Union Research Institute, 1970); Institute of International Relations, *Biography of Communist Chinese Leaders* (Taipei: Institute of International Relations, 1969); and Huang Chen-hsia, *Mao's Generals* (Hong Kong: Research Institute of Contemporary History, 1968).

14. Lin Piao, "Report to the Ninth National Congress of the Communist Party of China," *Peking Review,* no. 18 (April 30, 1969), p. 29.

15. *New China News Agency,* April 8, 1971.

16. Frederick C. Teiwes, *Provincial Party Personnel in Mainland China: 1956–1966* (New York: Occasional Papers of the East Asian Institute of Columbia University, 1967), pp. 22–23.

17. Ibid., p. 24.

18. Frederick C. Teiwes, *Provincial Leadership in China: The Cultural Revolution and Its Aftermath,* p. 94.

19. Ibid.

20. Ibid., p. 97.

21. Ibid., p. 98.

22. *People's Daily,* March 10, 1967.

23. See William Whitson, "The Field Army in Chinese Communist Military Politics," *The China Quarterly,* no. 37 (January/March 1969), pp. 3–15.

24. See John Gittings, *The Role of the Chinese Army* (New York: Oxford University Press, 1967), pp. 225–32.

25. Whitson, op. cit., p. 13.

# 6

## THE FALL
## OF LIN PIAO

No sooner had China begun to recover from its turbulent years, as political stability had been restored by the reestablishment of government and Party organizations at the national and provincial levels, than a series of highly unusual events occurred. Following the crash of a Chinese Air Force plane near the Soviet border in Outer Mongolia on September 13, 1971, all air traffic within China was banned for 58 hours. The traditional National Day (October 1) celebration in Tien An Men Square was abruptly canceled on September 22, even though construction and decoration of the reviewing stands was partially completed. Furthermore, radically departing from the past, no joint editorial was published to celebrate National Day, and pictures of Mao and Lin were conspicuously absent, indicating that something was definitely wrong.

Slowly, fragmentary information surfaced to reveal that another purge was underway, as extensive as the one which had barely ended. From October 1, 1971, the *New China News Agency* no longer mentioned Lin or any of his official titles (such as vice-chairman), and the *People's Daily* followed suit on October 2. Local broadcasting stations omitted all references to Lin as of October 8. In November, more information came from foreign sources. According to a Moscow broadcast, diplomatic missions in Peking received a notice to eliminate Lin's name from official greetings and toasts. In the November 29 telegram congratulating Albania on the forty-seventh anniversary of its liberation, Tung Pi-wu, in his capacity as vice-chairman of the People's Republic, replaced Lin Piao in the usual triad of signatures of Mao, Chou, and Lin.

At this juncture, a number of articles began to appear in major Chinese journals, attacking "plotters, conspirators, and traitors" in thinly veiled language without specifically mentioning names. Reportedly, Party cadres at the provincial level were informed of Lin's fall from favor by mid-October of 1971, and those at the basic levels by mid-November. Nevertheless, six months passed before Peking officially acknowledged Lin's purge to the outside world. On June 28 and July 10, 1972, Mao disclosed Lin's attempt to assassinate him to Ceylon's Prime Minister Sirimavo Bandaranaike and France's Foreign Minister Maurice Schumann, respectively.[1]

Another official explanation came from an unlikely part of the world, Algeria, where the Communist Chinese Embassy issued, on July 28, a statement in response to questions regarding the fate of Lin, describing him as

> a double-faced man ... [who] undertook antiparty activities in a planned, premeditated way with a well-determined program with the aim of taking over power, usurping the leadership of the Party, the Government and the army. ... He attempted a coup d'etat and tried to assassinate Mao Tse-tung. After his plot was foiled, he fled on September 12 towards the Soviet Union on a plane which crashed in the People's Republic of Mongolia.[2]

On the same day, Assistant Foreign Minister Wang Hai-jung, a close associate of Mao who reputedly speaks with indisputable authority, confirmed the validity of this report in Peking.

On October 7, 1972, Chou En-lai further clarified the mystery surrounding the grounding of all flights in China during September 1971; he disclosed to a delegation of the American Society of Newspaper Editors that Mao, deeply suspicious of Lin's motives in secretly arranging for an airplane to be readied with his son as pilot, had taken the drastic measure of halting all air traffic over China to frustrate Lin's possible escape by air. Nevertheless, according to Chou, Lin had managed to take off with his wife, son, and some close associates, but the plane crashed, while making a forced landing because of insufficient fuel, reportedly resulting in the death of Lin and the others.

## LIN'S ABORTIVE COUP

After October 1972, the following additional details about Lin's plot came to light. Official sources reported that on numerous past occasions Lin had openly defied Mao. One such instance occurred at the Ninth Party Congress when the new Party constitution was under consideration. Lin allegedly exerted pressure on Mao to declare Lin his official successor, in direct contradiction to the accepted practice of Communist parties. At the Second Plenum of the Ninth CC held at Lushan from August 23 to September 6, 1970, it was reported, Lin tried to ambush an unsuspecting Mao with a carefully planned and well-organized attack. Although this conference had originally been convened to discuss and approve economic policies, national defense strategies, and a draft revision of the state constitution, Lin had transformed it into an arena of confrontation between his forces and those of Mao, as Mao bitterly recalled:

> At this conference, they engaged in surprise attacks and underground activities. Why weren't they brave enough to come out in the open? It was obvious they were up to no good. First they concealed things, then they launched a surprise attack. They deceived three of the five standing members and the majority of comrades in the Politburo, except for the big generals. The big generals, including Huang Yung-sheng, Wu Fa-hsien, Yeh Ch'ün, Li Tso-p'eng, Ch'iu Hui-tso, and also Li Hsueh-feng and Cheng Wei-shan, maintained air-tight secrecy and suddenly launched a surprise attack. Their coup didn't just last a day and a half, but went on for two and a half days, from August 23 and August 24 to noon on the 25th. They certainly had a purpose in doing all that![3]

What Lin had planned to accomplish also seemed apparent to Mao:

> I thought that their surprise attacks and underground activity were planned, organized, and programmed. Their program was to set up a state chairman, advocate "genius," oppose the line set forth by 9th Party Congress, and overthrow the three items on the agenda of the Second Plenum of the 9th Central Committee. A certain person was very anxious to become state chairman, to split the Party, and to seize power. . . .[4]

Lin's view regarding the state chairmanship had directly opposed that of Mao who, while urging the convening of the Fourth People's Congress and the revision of the state constitution, had already recommended in March of 1970 that the position of state chairman (held last by Liu Shao-ch'i) be abolished. Furthermore, Mao claimed to have expressed his complete opposition by saying six times, "Do not establish a state chairman," and, "I will not be state chairman."[5] Therefore, in the draft of the state constitution presented to the Second Plenum of the Ninth CC and eventually adopted, Mao was designated as "the great leader of the people of all nationalities in the entire country, the Chief of State of the proletarian dictatorship, and the supreme commander of the whole nation and the whole armed forces,"[6] but the title "state chairman" was not mentioned.

The controversy surrounding Mao's "genius" had been a related but minor issue. In a speech to the Military Academy in 1967, Lin had said:

> Where will you find such mature thoughts as those of Mao Tse-tung? It will take the world hundreds of years, and China thousands of years, before one genius like Chairman Mao will appear. Chairman Mao is the greatest genius of this generation.[7]

Besides denying that he was in fact a "genius," Mao considered such adulation an abrogation of the role of the Party and the masses in the making of the revolution and an obvious attempt at flattery prompted by ulterior, selfish motives. As Mao put it: "He [Lin] said he wanted to build me up, but in fact I don't know who he had in mind—the truth is that he built up himself."[8] Continuing in a similar vein, Mao had construed a puzzling statement made by Lin at the height of the Cultural Revolution as equally self-serving:

> He also said that the People's Liberation Army was founded and led by me, but personally commanded by Lin—why can't the founder also command? As to the founding, it wasn't by me alone.[9]

After the Lushan Conference, Mao adopted three methods to undermine Lin's strength. In his characteristically folksy way of expressing himself, Mao described his methods as "throwing stones," "mixing in sand," and "digging up the cornerstone."[10] To "throw stones," in Mao's parlance, meant to attack some of Lin's prominent supporters or proteges. Thus, Mao initiated a nation-wide campaign to criticize Ch'en Po-ta, who had been accused of "deceiving" many people despite the fact that the MAC, dominated by Lin's followers, had already refused to find Ch'en guilty of the charges at an earlier meeting. Comparing the MAC to clay that is "too tightly packed that no air can get through," Mao then resorted to his second method, "mixing in sand," by adding new men whose personal loyalty was unquestioned. The third method, "digging up the cornerstone," refers to the reorganization of the Peking MR that took place toward the end of January 1971, as a result of an enlarged meeting of the Ninth CC at Peitaiho in north China in December 1970. Not only had Lin's Thirty-eighth Army, dispatched to Peking in 1966, now been removed;[11] but also, the commander of this MR, Cheng Wei-shan, and its political commissar, Li Hseuh-feng, were dismissed because of their intimate association with Lin. Lin's troops of the Fourth Field Army then stationed near Peking were transferred and replaced by the Third Field Army. With the removal of Lin's troops, north China had now come under the complete control of Mao.

Then in the latter half of February 1971, Lin Piao and his wife, Yeh Ch'ün, fully aware of their precarious position, reportedly sent their son, Lin Li-kuo, a deputy director of the Air Force Operations Department, to Shanghai and Hangchow to make plans for a coup d'etat. On March 20, Lin Li-kuo called a meeting in Shanghai to inform his supporters (Chou Yu-ch'ih, Yu Hsin-yeh, and Li Wei-hsin) that Lin Piao had given permission "to go ahead and draft a plan."[12] Therefore, from March 22 to 24, 1971, Lin Li-kuo and others reportedly labored on a document they called "An Outline of 'Project 571.' " (In Chinese, "571" or wu-ch'i-i is a homonym for military uprising.)

In April of 1971, the CC called another conference attended by 99 "responsible" cadres from national, local, and military units. This conference, often referred to as the "Conference of 99," might have set the stage for Lin's ouster. At the meeting Chou En-lai commented on the self-criticisms of the "big five" generals and those of Li Hsueh-feng and Cheng Wei-shan. And Mao, suspicious of Lin's future intentions, was reported to have voiced his doubts that the PLA would obey orders of rebellion:

> The army must be unified, must be put in order. I just don't believe that our army would rebel. I just don't believe that you, Huang Yung-sheng, could lead the Liberation Army to rebel. Each army includes divisions and regiments, and also commanding headquarters and political and logistics departments—if you order troops to do evil things, will they listen to you?[13]

In September 1971, Lin Piao and his men decided to implement "Project 571." The official version of what happened is as follows:

> Under Lin Piao's direct command, they tried in vain to assassinate Chairman Mao when he was making an inspection tour of the South, and at the same time murder Politburo comrades in Peking, so as to seize the top power of the Party and the state. After this counterrevolutionary plan went bankrupt, Lin Piao then plotted to take Yuang Yung-sheng, Wu Fa-hsien, Yeh Ch'un, Li Tso-p'eng, Ch'iu Hui-tso, and others to escape south to Canton and set up another central committee. However, actions taken by Chairman Mao torpedoed this arrangement by the Lin Piao anti-Party clique. Seeing his plot exposed and his fate sealed, Lin Piao then took his wife, son and a bunch of cohorts and hastily fled to an enemy country, thus turning into a traitor to the Party and the state. At 2:30 in the morning of September 13, 1971, the Trident jet No. 256, in which Lin and others took flight, crashed near Undur Khan in Mongolia. All those aboard, including Lin Piao, Yeh Ch'ün, and Lin Li-kuo, were burned to death. They died a renegade's and traitor's death, which was by no means enough to compensate for their crimes.[14]

In spite of the voluminous, and to a large extent, repetitious official announcements given so far to explain and justify the purge of Lin Piao, many critical questions remain unanswered. No reasonable explanation has been given regarding the discovery of the plot. "An Outline of 'Project 571' " is a naive, poorly written document by any standard. It is difficult to believe that Lin himself, a seasoned and battle-hardened veteran, could have been its author. Some observers conjecture that if in fact Lin Li-kuo wrote it, he might have done so without his father's knowledge or assistance, which might possibly account for its amateurish quality. Even more glaring in this alleged plan for a coup d'etat is the absence of any concrete operational details which would be essential to its implementation. The project resembles more than anything else a political diatribe against Mao. While the authenticity of the document has been established by experts, who remain somewhat puzzled as to its authorship, there is, nevertheless, the possibility that Peking might have altered or abridged the original version.

Many rumors circulated in Hong Kong suggesting that Lin, over 60 at the time, might not have died in the plane crash after all. Some of these speculations, all unsubstantiated, were that he was assassinated by secret agents at a conference in a manner analogous to the way in which L. P. Beria, the notorious head of the Soviet secret police under Stalin, met his death; that Lin was caught in the crossfire between his bodyguards and the troops of Wang Tung-hsing sent to arrest him; and that he was murdered before the flight and his body placed on the plane.

The most unconvincing of Lin's alleged crimes was the charge that he had engaged in "illicit relations" with foreign countries, presumably the Soviet Union. Yet, Lin's anti-Soviet attitude was well known, and there is little evidence that he had softened his basic distrust of Brezhnev and his comrades in later years. So far, only the "571" document can be cited as proof of Lin's treason. In it Lin claimed that "(b)ecause of the Maoist maltreatment of the Russians, our action will receive the support of the Soviet Union."[15] It is more likely that Lin simply quarreled with the policy of normalizing relations with the United States.[16]

## THE IMPACT OF THE PURGE OF LIN PIAO

The purge of Lin Piao had a far-reaching, profound impact on the factional politics of China. As has happened so frequently in the past to the followers of a fallen leader, Lin's close associates in the military, Party, and government were ousted.

When Lin fell, his suspected coconspirators fell with him. Removed from PLA General Headquarters were more than 33 high-level officers strategically situated in several key departments, in addition to Yeh Ch'ün (Lin's wife), who had managed to become the director of the General Office of the MAC of the CC. The chief of staff, Huang Yung-sheng, appointed by Lin in 1968, disappeared at the time that Lin's plot was uncovered and is presumed to have been purged, taking with him 6 of his 10 deputies (Wu Fa-hsien, Li Tso-p'eng, Ch'iu Hui-tso, Wen Yu-ch'eng, Yen Chung-ch'uan, and Chen Chi-te). The General Political Department, extensively reorganized in 1969 when Li Teh-sheng had been appointed its new director, was again reshuffled as a consequence of Lin's purge. Huang Chih-yung, a supporter of Lin Piao who had been named deputy director, was summarily dismissed in 1972. Ch'iu Hui-tso, the director of the

General Rear Services Department, was purged, and 7 of his 11 deputies shared his disgrace.*

Because of its extensive involvement in Lin's plot, the air force bore the brunt of the anti-Lin drive. The commander of the air force, Wu Fa-hsien, was one of the "big five" generals who were purged; also purged were 4 deputy commanders (Ts'eng Kuo-hua, Wang Ping-Chang, T'an Chia-shu, and Ho Chen-ya), 2 deputy political commissars (Liu Chin-p'ing and Yang Ching), 3 deputy chiefs of staff (Wang Fei, Hu P'ing, and Lu Min), and the deputy director of the War Department, Lin Li-kuo (Lin's son). Li Tso-p'eng, the first political commissar of the navy and deputy chief of staff, was purged, as well as a deputy commander (Chang Ching-yi) and a deputy political commissar (Chang Hsiu-ch'uan). Also stripped of their positions were the acting commander of the Armored Force, (Ch'en Hung), the deputy commander of the Signal Corps (Ch'en Wan-lan), the deputy commander of the Artillery (K'uang Yu-min), two deputy commanders (Wang T'ing and Yen Chia-an), and a deputy political commissar of the Second Artillery (Yu Ching-shan).

At the local level, the impact of Lin's purge was comparatively mild, giving credence to the observation that factional politics is more prevalent, or at least more conspicuous, at the national level. As far as can be ascertained, only 25 leaders in the MRs and MDs were purged because of their affiliation with Lin Piao. Ousted at the MR level were 2 commanders (Liang Hsing-ch'u and Lung Shu-chin), 6 deputy commanders (Wu Hsi-chih, Tuan Su-ch'uan, Wu Pao-shan, Wu Shui-shan, Yao Chi, and Lin Wei-hsien), and 2 first political commissars (Chou Ch'ih-p'ing and Liu Feng); at the MD level, 2 commanders (Yang Tung-liang and Hsiung Ying-t'ang), and 13 political commissars (Chang Ch'ao-jen, Nan P'ing, Ch'eng Shih-ch'ing, Wei Tsu-chen, Lan Yi-ning, Shih Hsin-an, Chang Yung-shen, Wang Hsin, Lu Yang, Ku Feng-ming, Yuan K'e-fu, Pu Chan-ya, and Han Te-fu).

Since many of the purged supporters of Lin Piao held positions in the NCC, the composition of this highest body of the CCP was naturally altered. The original Ninth CC regular membership of 170 was reduced to 143 after Lin's purge as a result of 9 deaths and 18 confirmed ousters; 7 of the Ninth CC alternates were removed, reducing total membership from 109 to 102. Of the 34 departures, 23 can be identified as military men, 10 as cadres; and one mass representative, Wang Chin-hsi, who died. In comparison with the original composition of the Ninth CC before Lin Piao's purge, the representation of the military dropped by 4.1 percent, while that of the cadres remained essentially the same. More importantly, not even one mass representative was

---

*Those purged included Han Chen-chi, Chou Yu-ch'eng, Chang Ming-yuan, Yen Chun, Wang Hsi-k'e, Chen P'ang, and T'ang T'ien-chi; the four deputy directors who remained, Chang Hsien-yueh, Chang Ling-pin, Chang T'ien-yun, and Feng Yung-shun.

purged because of Lin, and representation of this group went up by 3.7 percent because of the decrease in total membership, as shown by Table 3.

The impact of Lin's purge reached down to Party organizations at the provincial level, and all PPCs were partially reorganized because of it.* Thus, 8 first secretaries no longer retained their original appointments; those purged totalled 6 (Ch'eng Shih-ch'ing, Nan P'ing, Lung Shu-chin, Lan Yi-nung, Wang Chia-tao, and Liu Hsin-yuan); 2 died (Hsieh Fu-chih and Chang Kuo-hua). Second secretaries who were eliminated numbered three (Chou Ch-ih-p'ing, Liang Hsing-ch'u, and Liu Feng). And 9 secretaries were ousted (Yang Tung-liang, Cheng Ch'ao-jen, Ch'en Li-yun, Hsiung Ying-t'ang, Hsieh Cheng-jung, P'u Chan-ya, Wei Tsu-chen, Wang Hsin, and Chang Yung-shen). The decline of military representation in the CC was paralleled in the PPCs. While 21 of the 29 original PPC first secretaries could be described as military and eight as cadres, only 13 military and 12 cadres (including one acting secretary) were among the 25 known first secretaries.

The purge of Lin Piao also affected the organization of the RCs, for many of Lin's followers had held concurrent positions in the RCs when these orga-

### TABLE 3

### Comparison of the Composition of the Ninth Central Committee Before and After Lin Piao's Purge

|  | Period | | |
|  | Before Purge | After Purge | Change |
|---|---|---|---|
| Total | | | |
| Members | 279 | 245 | −34 |
| Military | | | |
| Number | 123 | 100 | −23 |
| Percent | 44.1 | 40.1 | − 4.1 |
| Cadres | | | |
| Number | 73 | 63 | −10 |
| Percent | 26.1 | 25.7 | − 0.4 |
| Masses | | | |
| Number | 83 | 82 | − 1 |
| Percent | 29.7 | 33.4 | + 3.7 |

Source: Based on data from Chung-kung yen-chiu, Chung-kung nien-pao, and Fei-ch'ing yueh-pao.

---

*The five PPCs which suffered the least turnover in personnel were Shanghai, Tientsin, Ninghsia, Shantung, and Kiangsu.

nizations ruled the provinces with concentrated power at the height of the Cultural Revolution. In addition to 2 who died (Hsieh Fu-chih and Chang Kuo-hua), 12 RC chairmen were purged because of their collaboration with Lin. This group included 6 first secretaries of PPCs (Lung Shu-chin, Nan P'ing, Ch'eng Shih-ch'ing, Liu Hsin-yuan, Lan Yi-ning, and Wang Chia-tao), and 4 others (Wang Hsiao-yu, Liu Ke-p'ing, Teng Hai-ch'ing, and Li Yuan).

## Replacements for the Fallen Linists

The purge of Lin Piao and his clique necessitated the restaffing and, on occasion, the reorganization of the military, government, and Party power structures. In the ensuing two years, Peking moved slowly in naming replacements, with many crucial posts simply left unfilled. Although Yeh Chien-ying, a semiretired marshal in his mid-seventies, assumed the position of acting minister of national defense and acting vice-chairman of the MAC as part of an effort to resuscitate the partially paralyzed national military command, the vital post of chief of staff (last held by the purged Huang Yung-sheng), as well as the less important positions of director of the General Rear Services, first political commissar of the Navy, and commanders of the Armored Force and Second Artillery, were left vacant for several years.

The central leadership initiated a program of gradual "liberation" of military leaders criticized during the Cultural Revolution or victimized by Lin. Of the 39 replacements identifiable by 1973, 12 could be said to have been liberated and, more significantly, all of these were given important assignments.* Clearly discernible also was the center's conscious effort to distribute new assignments among the major field army systems in such a fashion as to avoid a repetition of the one-faction domination which had occurred under Lin. Though in 1973 the Fourth Field Army still enjoyed a slight predominance, the leadership of other field armies began to clamor for their share of choice assignments. Fifteen (40 percent) of the 39 replacements whose army affiliation was known came from the Fourth Field Army; the Third and First Field Armies claimed 9 and 6, respectively; and the Second Field Army, 3.

In the PPCs, there was again an apparent attempt to use liberated cadres

---

*These were Yang Yung (commander of Sinkiang MR); Lo K'un-shan (deputy commander of Shenyang MR); Yi Yueh (deputy political commissar of Lanchow MR); Chang Tsung-sun (deputy commander of Tsinan MR); Li Chih-min (first political commissar of Foochow MR); Ch'en Tsai-tao (deputy commander of Foochow MR); Chung Han-hua (deputy political commissar of Canton MR); P'eng Chia-ch'ing (deputy political commissar of Canton MR); Ts'eng Yung-ya (deputy commander of Shenyang MR); T'an Ch'i-lung (first political commissar of Chekiang MD); Chang Chen (deputy commander of Wuhan MR); and Yen Chih-shan (political commissar of Shensi MD).

to replace those purged because of their association with Lin; 16 of the 17 new secretaries and deputy secretaries of the PCs named by early 1973 fell into this category. Another significant development was decreased military representation among the new replacements. Of the new 17 PPC officials, 8 were cadres, but only 5 could be identified as military men. The same phenomenon was evident when new RC chairmen were appointed, of whom there were 9 by early 1973. Most purged RC chairmen had come from the ranks of the military; however, 5 cadres (Wu Teh, Saifudin, Hua Kuo-feng, Li Ta-chang, and T'an Ch'i-lung), as opposed to only 4 military figures (Yu Tai-chung, Hsieh Chen-hua, Ting Sheng, and Yang Te-chih), replaced them. The decline in military dominance in the RCs, coupled with a corresponding increase in cadre influence, is striking when the professional backgrounds of all RC chairmen are considered; 13 chairmen from military backgrounds, instead of the previous 21, now hold office, while the number of cadres has increased from 8 to 11.

To summarize, Lin's plot to assassinate Mao not only spelled Lin's demise but also resulted in a purge of his supporters at the national and provincial levels. Since most were members of the military establishment, the representation of this group in the CC, PPCs, and RCs was subsequently reduced. As the soldiers left the scene, cadres returned to fill the vacuum. More significantly, many cadres purged by Lin now were liberated and reappointed to posts vacated by Lin's men. These developments, beginning immediately after Lin's fall, continued when the Tenth Party Congress convened.

## NOTES

1. *Agence France-Press,* July 27, 1972.

2. *New York Times,* July 29, 1972.

3. "Top-secret Document of the Central Committee of the Chinese Communist Party" (*Chung-fa,* no. 12, 1972), cited in *Chinese Law and Government,* Fall–Winter 1972–73, p. 35.

4. Ibid., pp. 35–36.

5. Ibid., p. 37.

6. Article 2 of "Text of the 1970 Draft of the Revised Constitution of the People's Republic of China," in *Studies in Comparative Communism 4,* no. 1 (January 1971), p. 100.

7. Institute for the Study of Chinese Communist Problems, *Important CCP Documents of the Great Proletarian Cultural Revolution* (Taipei: Institute for the Study of Chinese Communist Problems, 1973), p. 367.

8. *Chinese Law and Government,* Fall–Winter 1972–73, p. 38.

9. Ibid.

10. Ibid.

11. See Y. M. Kau and P. M. Perrolle, "The Politics of Lin Piao's Abortive Military Coup," *Asian Survey 14,* June 1974, p. 561.

12. "Top-secret Document of the Central Committee of the Chinese Communist Party" (*Chung-fa,* no. 4, 1972), cited in *Chinese Law and Government,* Fall–Winter 1972–73, p. 46.

13. "Document of the Central Committee of the Chinese Communist Party" (*Chung-fa,* no. 12, 1972), in ibid., p. 39.

14. "Top-secret Document of the Central Committee of the Chinese Communist Party" (*Chung-fa*, no. 24, 1972), cited in ibid., p. 64.

15. See *Issues and Studies 8,* no. 8, May 1972, p. 80.

16. See Philip Bridgham, "The Fall of Lin Piao," *The China Quarterly,* no. 55 (July/ September 1973), p. 446.

# 7

## THE TENTH PARTY CONGRESS
## AND ITS AFTERMATH

The Tenth Party Congress was held in Peking from August 24 to 28, 1973. Like the Ninth, it received no advance publicity despite the fact that delegates were elected to this important gathering as early as May 1973.[1] The Party Congress was again convened in strict secrecy, and announcements that it had actually taken place were made only after its adjournment.

There were other irregularities as well. Although a plenum of the CC is usually called to make preparations for a coming national Party Congress, no plenum was assembled to settle the preliminaries for the Tenth Congress. This constituted a glaring variation from past practices, since the Seventh Plenum of the Seventh CC had met two weeks before the Eighth Party Congress was held, and the Twelfth Plenum of the Eighth CC had met three months before the Ninth Party Congress. Yet the Third Plenum of the Ninth Party Committee, anticipated by many to preceed the Tenth Party Congress, had never occurred, although a "Central Work Conference"[2] was convened in May, which considered "41 drafts"[3] of constitutional amendments from Party organizations at the lower levels.

The session of the Tenth Congress was extremely brief in comparison with those of the Eighth and Ninth Congresses, which had lasted 13 and 24 days, respectively. It seems doubtful that a thorough discussion of any of the items on the agenda[4] could have been possible in a period of only five days. The Congress probably performed no other function than that of simply rubber-stamping the proposals already thrashed out in advance.

Finally, past Party Congresses were generally postponed beyond the time stipulated by the Party Constitutions. According to the constitution adopted by the Seventh Party Congress, a Party congress "shall be convened once in every three years" (Article 29), but the Eighth Party Congress had not been convened until September, 1956, eleven and a half years later. Twelve and a half years elapsed before the Ninth Party Congress had taken place, even though the revised constitution of the Eighth Party Congress had specified that a Party Congress should meet "every five years" (Chapter III). The Tenth Party Congress, meeting only four years and five months after the Ninth, was in fact the first national congress in the history of the CCP to be convened earlier than prescribed.

All these highly unusual developments (the secrecy of the Tenth Party Congress, the absence of a plenum to make preparations, the brevity of the session, and the premature convocation) cannot be fully explained on the basis of presently available information. Some have attributed them to large-scale dissension which was said to prevail in Peking not only over the substantive issues a conference of this nature would be expected to settle, but even on the appropriateness of calling a meeting at this particular time.[5]

## OFFICIAL DENUNCIATION OF LIN PIAO AND HIS CLIQUE

According to Article 8 of the Ninth Party Constitution, a Party congress could be convened earlier than prescribed only under "special circumstances," which in this instance was certainly the Lin Piao incident. Two years had passed during which China remained officially silent on the purge of Lin. Peking obviously felt that a new Party Congress would provide the ideal occasion to present its formal explanation of what had happened, eradicate any remaining traces of Lin's influence, and restructure the power apparatus of China.

In his report to the Tenth Congress, Chou En-lai disclosed that Lin's draft of the political report to the Ninth Congress, prepared in collaboration with Ch'en Po-ta, had opposed "continuing the revolution" and instead contended that "to develop production" was "the main task"[6] for the years ahead, echoing the line of Liu Shao-ch'i. Only after the CC had rejected his version did Lin "grudgingly" read the one "drawn up under Chairman Mao's personal guidance"[7] to the congress. In his report, Chou identified Lin Piao as one of those who "never showed up without a copy of the 'Quotations' in hand and never opened his mouth without shouting 'long live' and who spoke nice things to your face but stabbed you in the back."[8] Chou also formally confirmed the existence of "Project 571" without revealing additional information and reiterated the earlier accusations against Lin, who was now expelled from the Party "once for all."[9]

## THE TENTH CENTRAL COMMITTEE

The Tenth CC, was elected at the congress, consisting of 195 regular and

124 alternate members, a 40-member increase over the Ninth CC. Like its predecessor, the Tenth CC continued the implementation of "getting rid of the stale and taking in the fresh."[10] Thus, 35 of the 170 regular Ninth CC members were not reelected and 3 were demoted to alternate status,[11] while 10 had died.[12] Fifty-five, or 28.2 percent, became regular CC members for the first time. The turnover was even more striking among the alternate members of the Tenth CC, where those newly elected totaled 58, or 46.7 percent. While 18 of the 109 Ninth CC alternates were promoted to regular status, 28 were dropped.

The persecution of Lin Piao's clique was evident in the Tenth CC; 22 of the 35 regulars and 15 of the 28 alternates not reelected can be classified as Lin's accomplices. Some of Lin's supporters, such as Ting Sheng, Liu Hsing-yuan, and Han Hsien-ch'u, still retained their seats in the Tenth CC, but their importance as a viable political group is rapidly diminished. The purge of Lin's faction has resulted in a drop in the percentage of military representation; 52 of the 73 Ninth CC members not reelected can be identified as military personnel, while only 17 cadres and 4 mass representatives suffered such a loss. Furthermore, their replacements in most cases have not come from the military establishment. Of the 92 new members of the Tenth CC whose back-

## TABLE 4

### Comparison of the Composition of the Ninth and Tenth Central Committees

|  | Central Committee | | Change |
|---|---|---|---|
|  | Ninth | Tenth |  |
| Total |  |  |  |
| Members | 279 | 319 | +40 |
| Military |  |  |  |
| Number | 123 | 100 | −23 |
| Percent | 44.1 | 31.3 | −12.8 |
| Cadres |  |  |  |
| Number | 73 | 91 | +18 |
| Percent | 26.1 | 28.5 | + 2.4 |
| Masses |  |  |  |
| Number | 83 | 128* | +45 |
| Percent | 29.7 | 40.1 | +10.4 |

*Includes 21 members whose backgrounds are unknown.

*Source:* Based on data from *Chung-kung yen-chiu, Chung-kung nien-pao,* and *Fei-ch'ing yueh-pao.*

grounds are known, representatives of the military and the masses numbered 28 each, but the cadre group scored the largest gain with 36 members. Among the 319 members of the Tenth CC, 100 (31.3 percent) can be described as professional soldiers; 91 (28.5 percent), as cadres; and 107 (33.5 percent), as mass representatives. Most of the 21 members whose backgrounds cannot be ascertained may also represent the masses, since scattered pieces of information suggest that they were relatively young and probably come from factories and communes, accounting for their present obscurity. Having proven their loyalty to the radical goals of the Cultural Revolution, they could easily be the leaders of new recruits, who comprise 25 percent of the 28 million Party members.[13] If these 21 members are added to the mass representatives, the number of this group's representation in the Tenth CC could climb as high as 128, or 40.1 percent. Contrasting the composition of the Ninth CC with that of the Tenth, the percentage of cadres remained almost constant, while that of the military decreased by 12.8 percent, and that of the masses rose by 10.4 percent, as Table 4 shows.

The number of members in the Tenth Politburo has remained the same as that of the Ninth CC—21. All Ninth Politburo members, except Lin's coconspirators and Hsieh Fu-chih, who died, were reelected. Of the 4 alternates of the Ninth Politburo, only 1, Li Hsueh-feng, was purged; the other 3 were elevated to the status of regular member (Chi Teng-k'uei, Wang Tung-hsing and Li Teh-sheng). All 8 purged were connected in one way or another with the military. Further, 9 new members were elected to replace those eliminated; all can be categorized as cadres with the exception of Su Chen-hua, a naval officer who was chosen as 1 of 4 new alternates. Thus, the Tenth Politburo mirrored the decline in military representation and rise of the cadre group (previously noted at the CC level), as shown in Table 5.

The Standing Committee of the Tenth Politburo was expanded from 5 to 9 members, and Mao Tse-tung, as was to be expected, retained the chairmanship. For unknown reasons, 6 new members were added to replace the 2 purged, Lin Piao and Ch'en Po-ta. Yeh Chien-ying, Chu Teh, Chang Ch'un-ch'iao, and Tung Pi-wu had already served as members of the Ninth Politburo, and they were joined by Li Teh-sheng, previously an alternate, and Wang Hung-wen, only a regular of the Ninth CC.

The number of vice-chairmen was increased from 1, Lin Piao, to 5 in the Tenth CC—Chou En-lai, Wang Hung-wen, K'ang Sheng, Yeh Chien-ying, and Li Teh-sheng. Since they are not listed according to the number of strokes in their surnames, the new ordering was a subtle indication of their relative status and ranking.

That Chou would be listed as the second most important person in the Party was not surprising, but Wang Hung-wen (the new holder of the number 3 position), entrusted with the coveted assignment of delivering the report on the revision of the Party Constitution to the Tenth Party Congress, could be called a classic example of a dark horse. A demobilized PLA veteran who had worked in the security section of the Shanghai Cotton Factory no. 17 before the Cultural Revolution, Wang had been instrumental in organizing several million workers to form the "headquarters of Shanghai workers" against the Party establishment in 1967. Because of his exemplary efforts in the radical cause, Wang had attracted the attention of Chang Ch'un-ch'iao and Yao Wen-yuan, and when both later went to Peking, Wang, a secretary, actually ran the MPC of Shanghai in their absence. A regular member of the Ninth CC, Wang was summoned to the capital in September 1972 and assigned an important but unspecified position in the Party CC.[14] There was some speculation that he became the head of the organization department of the Party.[15]

Ranked immediately beneath Wang, K'ang Sheng is a security chief and member of the Standing Committee of the Ninth Politburo. Yeh Chien-ying's ascendency to a vice-chairmanship could be attributed not only to his membership in the Ninth Politburo but also to his role as Chou's most trusted and helpful lieutenant. However, the dramatic elevation of Li Teh-sheng was unexpected, since Li had been only an alternate member of the Ninth Politburo and obscure provincial military commander from Anhwei before his subsequent appointment as director of the General Political Department of the PLA.

TABLE 5

### Comparison of the Composition of the Ninth and Tenth Politburos

|  | Politburo | | Change |
|---|---|---|---|
|  | Ninth | Tenth |  |
| Total |  |  |  |
| Members | 21* | 21* | 0 |
| Military |  |  |  |
| Number | 12 | 6 | − 6 |
| Percent | 60 | 30 | −30 |
| Cadres |  |  |  |
| Number | 4 | 6 | + 2 |
| Percent | 20 | 30 | +10 |
| Masses |  |  |  |
| Number | 4 | 8 | + 4 |
| Percent | 20 | 40 | +20 |

*Mao not included.

*Source:* Based on data from *Chung-kung yen-chiu, Chung-kung nien-pao,* and *Fei-ch'ing yueh-pao.*

## COALITION CHANGES AND FACTIONAL REALIGNMENTS

With Lin Piao gone and their preeminent role in the Tenth CC severely curtailed, the military has suffered a substantial setback and their influence appeared to wane. Nevertheless, as a group, they were still very much entrenched in the Party, evidenced by the fact that every leading figure in the PLA headquarters was elected to the Tenth CC.[16] Moreover, with the exception of 3 political commissars (Yuan Sheng-p'ing (Tsinan MR), Yeh Cheng (Chengtu MR), and Ts'ao Ssu-ming (Sinkiang MR)), the commanders and political commissars of the 11 MRs were selected for positions in the new CC. In short, the military still wielded considerable power, which they could bring to bear in future controversies.

Party cadres, the main beneficiaries of the decline of the military, regained their lost strength. As pointed out earlier, fewer cadres in the Ninth CC were initially purged and proportionately more cadres were elected to the Tenth CC than any other group. What is more significant, however, is the fact that of the 113 new members of the Tenth CC, more than 40 regulars and 12 alternates (46 percent) were liberated cadres who had previously been criticized and in some cases removed from their positions of power. Since the purge of Lin, some have returned to public life. The most dramatic example was Teng Hsiao-p'ing; his resurrection has not been convincingly explained by the central authorities and remains one of the more perplexing mysteries of the Cultural Revolution.

At a banquet given by Chou En-lai on April 12, 1973, for Prince Sihanouk and his wife, who had just returned from a visit to Cambodia, Teng was seen in public for the first time since he had been purged. To the applause of those invited, he was introduced by Chou as a vice-premier of the State Council, the position he had held before the Cultural Revolution; more significantly, Teng, who looked ill, was assisted by Wang Hai-jung, Mao's niece and one of Teng's most vocal attackers during the early stages of the Cultural Revolution, an indication that Mao either approved of or at least acquiesced to his reappearance.

Other well-known Liuists previously purged but later turned to public life included Li Ching-ch'uan, first secretary of the CC's Southwest Bureau and first political commissar of the Chengtu MR, who had been dismissed in May 1967 for "adamantly implementing the Liu-Teng (Shao-chi—Hsiao-p'ing) line and turning Szechwan province into an 'independent kingdom' which is anti-Party, anti-socialism and anti-Mao Tse-tung's thoughts";[17] T'an Chen-lin, a vice-premier, who had been condemned as a "traitor"[18] for organizing the "February Adverse Current" in an attempt to reverse the verdict on Liu and Teng;[19] and Ulanfu, a vice-premier and first secretary of the Inner Mongolia Party Committee who had been purged in April 1967 for "disobeying orders from the Central Committee and the MAC."[20]

Increased cadre representation in the Tenth CC, coupled later with the return of those liberated, seemed to substantiate the observation at that point that Chou En-lai, whose support had come mainly from the bureaucracy and whose moderate and pragmatic policies had been most responsible for the liberation of many previously purged, appeared to be on the rise. The elimination of Lin left Chou the second most powerful man in China next to Chairman Mao himself.

Nevertheless, under more careful scrutiny, Chou's power base, dependent mainly on the support of pragmatists in the bureaucracy and military establishment, was more fragile than one first realizes. Unlike Lin Piao, who had been made the first and only vice-chairman of the Party at the ninth congress, Chou was but one of five vice-chairmen, even though his name appeared before the other four in the official roster, suggesting that he was regarded as "first among equals." In the Standing Committee of the Tenth Politburo, Chou could claim Yeh Chien-ying, Ch Teh, and Tung Pi-wu as potential allies, but all three were then quite old, and in the case of Chu and Tung, essentially inactive. Moreover, Chou's followers formed a minority in the Politburo and were much in need of uncommitted votes.[21] While it was true that three of Chou's key aides in the Ministry of Foreign Affairs were elected to the CC for the first time (Chi P'eng-fei, then foreign minister; Ch'iao Kuan-hua, Chi's principal deputy; and Huang Hua, China's permanent delegate to the United Nations), and one was reelected to the Tenth CC (Huang Chen, head of the Chinese Liaison Office in Washington), the representation of the State Council in the Tenth CC remained at 10 percent[22]—the same as in the Ninth CC but 15 percent less than in the Eighth.[23] Although nearly half of the newly elected members of the Tenth CC were liberated cadres, most had not yet regained their former positions, and it may be some time before they again play a role commensurate with their previous seniority and experience. All in all, while Chou and those who had supported him gained in strength in comparison with the time that Lin Piao was in power, nevertheless, they now had to contend with the potentially formidable capabilities of the leftists if polarizing disagreements over policies occurred in the future.

At first glance, the radicals did not fare well in the Tenth CC, since such key figures as Chiang Ch'ing, Yao Wen-yuan, and Chang Ch'un-ch'iao failed to make discernible advances in the Party hierarchy. Chiang did not advance to the Standing Committee of the Politburo even though four new members were added. In fact, her Party rank dropped noticeably during the brief session of the Tenth Congress.[24] Yao, widely heralded after Lin's purge as the most likely successor to Mao, failed to obtain additional responsibility and stature other than membership in the Politburo, which he had held before. Chang Ch'un-ch'iao also underwent an unexpected loss in prestige. If past precedent were observed, Chang, as the secretary-general of the Tenth Congress, should have assumed a parallel position in the Party secretariat, which had been dissolved during the Cultural Revolution; however, for reasons unknown, its expected revival never materialized.

But the temporary eclipse of the leftists has been more than offset by the new status of Li Teh-sheng and the spectacular rise of Wang Hung-wen. Another Party vice-chairman, K'ang Sheng, could be included in this group as well. In the Standing Committee of the Politburo, the radicals divided the seats equally with supporters of Chou, excluding Mao as the ninth member, but in the Politburo itself, they claimed at least 10 of the 21 members. The principal strength of the leftists was in the CC as a whole, since a majority of mass representatives belonged to this group.

## THE QUESTION OF SUCCESSION

The struggle to succeed Mao, by then 80, which had originated in the Cultural Revolution and intensified after the purge of Lin Piao, was not resolved by the Tenth Party Congress, for no successor was officially named. Twice betrayed previously by a chosen heir, Mao was now probably too wary to select a third. Wang may have voiced Mao's preference when he recommended in his report that "not just one or two persons" but "millions" of successors should be trained:[25]

> Many elder comrades expressed the strong desire that we must further improve the work of training successors. . . . Many young comrades on their part warmly pledged to learn modestly from the strong points of veteran cadres . . . to be strict with themselves and to do their best to carry on the revolution.[26]

In fact, this new emphasis on youthful successors was reflected in the new Party constitution, which clearly stated:

> The leading bodies of the Party at all levels shall be elected . . . in accordance with the requirements for successors to the cause of the proletarian revolution and the principle of combining the old, the middle-aged and the young.[27]

Admittedly, senior cadres—survivors of the Long March—still dominated the highest Party organs, but younger leaders of the World War II generation succeeded in achieving token representation. In the Standing Committee of the Politburo, Wang Hung-wen was under 40, Chang Ch'un-ch'iao was about 50, and Li Teh-sheng was around 56, while the average age of the remaining six members was over 70. Wang, again, is the only member in the 21-man Politburo under 40; six are under 60, and fourteen are over that age.[28]

In the CC itself, however, the percentage of younger men increased sharply among the full members and even more dramatically among the alternates.

Given this new emphasis on youth, Mao's successor will probably come from a group of men in their fifties, but in terms of both experience and national stature, none so far qualifies for the chairmanship of the CCP. It may be some time after a period of collective rule before a new supreme leader emerges.

## REALIGNMENTS IN THE MILITARY REGIONS

If the Cultural Revolution had eroded the Party's control over the regional commanders, who have been called the "main beneficiaries of the collapse of the Party apparatus,"[29] the Party obviously felt sufficiently secure to correct the imbalance after the Tenth Congress. In a surprise move on January 1, 1974, China belatedly announced the completion of the reassignment of eight commanders of the 11 MRs, which had begun sometime in mid-December. This was the most sweeping and extensive reshuffle since 1954, when the military administrative structure of the country had first been subdivided into 13 MRs.

Among the MR commanders reassigned, Hsu Shih-yu (Nanking) and Ting Sheng (Canton) exchanged posts, as did Yang Te-chih (Lanchow) and Han Hsien-ch'u (Foochow). Ch'en Hsi-lien, the commander of Shenyang MR, was reassigned to command the Peking MR, whose ex-commander, Cheng Wei-shan, a supporter of Lin Piao, had been disgraced in late 1970 on grounds of "disobedience"; and Li Teh-sheng was sent to Manchuria as Ch'en's replacement.

For all practical purposes, this amounted to a complete overhaul of the structure of the MRs after the purge of Lin Piao, since the only three commanders not reassigned (Yang Yung (Sinkiang MR), Ch'in Chi-wei (Chengtu MR), and Wang Pi-ch'eng (Kunming MR)), had been appointed after Lin's downfall. The continued oppression of Lin's men was obvious by the reassignment of two remaining commanders who had belonged to the Lin faction, Tseng Ssu-yu and Han Hsien-ch'u, to posts of lesser importance.*

As the Fourth Field Army fell out of favor, the Third Field Army assumed the mantle of favored son, for as soon as Lin had disappeared from the scene, elements of the Third Field Army moved into Peking to begin garrison

---

*Both in terms of size and importance, the new assignments of Tseng Ssu-yu and Han Hsien-ch'u, Tsinan MR and Lanchow MR, respectively, were less significant than their original posts, Wuhan MR and Foochow MR, respectively.

duties; it is understandable that Chou En-lai trusted and relied heavily on this military faction, which his close friend, Ch'en Yi, had once commanded. The puzzling reassignment of Ch'en Hsi-lien from Shenyang MR, where he had been stationed for more than 14 years, to the Peking MR can be attributed to Chou's preference of having a close colleague in control of the nation's capital. Far from being deprived of the commanding post in an admittedly sensitive area bordering the Soviet Union, Ch'en may actually have been selected for a strategic position in the central military establishment, and his new post should be taken as an expression of confidence by the central authorities.

Equally mystifying was the assignment of Hsu Shih-yu, commander of the Nanking MR since 1954, who was dispatched to the Canton MR—a traditional territorial base of the Fourth Field Army. One theory is that since Hsu had once opposed Mao during the Yenan period and defied him during the Cultural Revolution, his new assignment should be regarded as a demotion of a punitive nature.[30] On the other hand, Hau had been a loyal supporter of Chou, and it is quite plausible that Chou sent him to Canton in order to maintain close surveillance over the Fourth Field Army.

The assigning of Li Teh-sheng, the director of the Political Department of the PLA since September 1970 and a newly elected vice-chairman of the Party's CC at the Tenth Congress, to an MR was highly unusual and unprecedented. Li's connection with the CCRG was well known, and he may have fallen out of favor as Chou En-lai strengthened his control over the nation's military.

Another probable reason for this military reorganization was to reduce the dominance of the military at the local level. The reassignments of the commanders to other regions, including those who had been stationed in certain areas for prolonged periods (Hsu Shih-yu had commanded the Nanking MR since 1954 and Yang Te-chih the Tsinan MR for almost 16 years), were probably aimed at decreasing their strong local ties and support resulting from years of entrenched rule, as well as eliminating "mountain strongholds" where the commanders could rule as virtual sovereigns.

The rearrangement of commanders also accomplished the unpublicized goal of stripping them of their Party positions in the local power structure. Before the Cultural Revolution, the posts of commander of MRs and MDs, first secretary of PCs, or governor of a province had never been given to any one person. When the disruption of the Cultural Revolution then rendered the Party committees and governmental organizations impotent, much power gravitated into the hands of the military commanders. In addition to their military duties, they became chairmen of the RCs, as well as first secretaries of the PPCs. It is important to point out that with the exception of P'i Ting-chun, all of the commanders involved in the shakeup have been both chairmen of RCs and first secretaries of the PPCs. In their present locales, they no longer can hold any concurrent Party and governmental positions. The three commanders who were not moved had been appointed after the purge of Lin and have held strictly military positions, as commanders of MRs only.

## THE ANTI-CONFUCIUS AND ANTI-LIN CAMPAIGNS

The anti-Confucius campaign, launched during the latter part of 1973, was a continuation of the attack on the rightists. Considered the "venerable master" of Liu Shao-ch'i,[31] Confucius, whose philosophies have underpinned the Chinese political and social systems for more than two thousand years, was condemned for "frantically calling for the restoration and preservation of the slave system and for the consolidation of the slave-owning, aristocratic class."[32] Repugnant to communist philosophy was the Confucian teaching that "those who labor with their minds govern others; those who labor with their strength are governed by others,"[33] which had supported class distinctions as well as denigrated the importance of manual labor. Singled out for criticism also were many concepts first espoused by Confucius, such as "virtue," "benevolence and righteousness," "loyalty and forbearance," and "doctrine of the mean."

In early 1974 Mao "initiated and led"[34] the movement to link the anti-Confucius campaign with a new nationwide assault on Lin Piao, who was called "an out-and-out disciple of Confucius,"[35] whose "inner world" was "foul and ugly."[36] Lin's misdeeds, according to study materials used in this campaign and released by the Chinese in January 1974, were arranged into eight categories supported by allegedly corroborating evidence.

First, Lin had been guilty of quoting extensively from the Confucian *Analects*, such as his use of the phrase "to restrain oneself and restore the rites," in scrolls written for his wife in 1969 and 1970 and hung in their bedroom.[37] His wife had also written a scroll using the same expression. According to the official explanatory note, "to restrain oneself and restore the rites" was a "Confucian reactionary program for restoring the slave system," and both Lin and his wife had "fully exposed their anxious ambition to subvert the dictatorship of the proletariat, and to regard the restoration of capitalism as the most important of all things."[38] Furthermore, in the *Chung-fa* Document no. 24 (1972), Lin, in objecting to Mao's wish not to maintain the position of state chairman, had again quoted Confucius by saying that if a country has no official head, "there will be no right titles and words will not be proper."[39]

Second, in another scroll, written in 1962, Lin had compared himself to a "heavenly horse" and implied that he was a "man above men."[40] This clearly showed the influence of Mencius, who said:

> If it [Heaven] wished this [that the kingdom should enjoy tranquility and good order], who is there besides me to bring about it?[41]

And "The Outline of 'Project 571' " had contained the passage, "The leadership of the revolution has historically fallen on our fleet (the code name for Lin's forces),"[42] paralleling the Confucian saying, "Heaven produced the virtue that is in me. Hwan T'ui (Minister of War of the State of Sung)—what can he do to me?"[43] Lin's acceptance of "genius," a particularly sensitive point to Mao, was an obvious outgrowth of his belief that some men are predestined to be heroes. Lin had said in a talk to an enlarged meeting of the Politburo on May 18, 1966:

> Some people do not believe that there are geniuses. That is not Marxism. One has to believe that there are geniuses.[44]

In a later speech, on September 18, 1966, Lin had added:

> ... such a genius can emerge in the whole world only every several hundred years; and in China, only every several thousand years.[45]

The study materials linked Lin's statements with the following section from Confucius:

> Those who are born with the possession of knowledge are the highest class of men. Those who learn and get possession of knowledge are the next. Those who are dull and stupid and yet compass the learning, are another class next to these. As to those who are dull and stupid and yet do not learn—they are the lowest of the people.[46]

The following words of Mencius were also found relevant:

> It is a rule that a true royal sovereign should arise in the course of five hundred years, and that during that time there should be men illustrious in their generation.[47]

Third, in *Chung-fa* Document no. 4 (1972), there had been the statement, attributed to the Lin "gang," that "The heroes and the slaves jointly created history"; this had been derived from Mencius, who said:

> If there were not men of a superior grade, there would be none to rule the countrymen. If there were not countrymen, there would be none to support the men of superior grade.[48]

In fact, Lin's disdain for the common people had been evident in many of his speeches. At the Seventh Party Congress of May 1945, he had said:

> The people are not talking every day about the resistance against Japan. ...

They are thinking of the whole business of their livelihood and we are thinking of the whole business of ours.

What the common peasants and workers think about is how to make money, how to get some rice, edible oil, salt, sauce, vinegar and firewood, and their wives, sons and daughters. . . . Our thoughts are entirely different from theirs. . . . The difference between our thoughts and theirs is that between heaven and earth.[49]

Because of his feelings of innate superiority, Lin was quoted as having said, at the Central Work Conference on August 13, 1966, "One must carry out what he understands, as well as what he doesn't understand,"[50] a statement similar to a remark of Confucius, who said, "The people may be made to follow a path of action, but they may not be made to understand it."[51]

Fourth, at the Second Plenum of the Eighth Party Congress on May 8, 1958, Lin had condemned the Emperor Ch'in Shih Huang for "burning books and burying scholars alive,"[52] and had urged everyone, in a speech delivered on August 8, 1966, to "become a Tung Chung-shu," the "purest" Confucian scholar who lived during the Han dynasty when all other schools were banned.[53] In a 1969 scroll for his wife, Lin had indirectly criticized Mao by saying, "Those who rely on virtue will thrive and those who rely on force will perish."[54] This was taken from the *Shih Chi* or *Historical Records,* and closely resembles the words of Mencius:

When one subdues men by force, they do not submit to him in heart. . . . When one subdues men by virtue, in their hearts' core they are pleased and sincerely submit.[55]

Fifth, Lin had told his wife, on March 13, 1970, "The Doctrine of the Mean [is] rational," praising the Confucian doctrine, "Perfect is the virtue which is according to the Constant Mean."[56] And Yeh Ch'ün observed, in this regard:

Things should not be carried to the extreme. To go to the extreme is the theory of one point and will create evil consequences. If the consequences are great, they will be revealed; if the consequences are small, or can be suppressed by other forces, they will not be revealed. (But one must boldly assume that there must be evil consequences.)[57]

Sixth, Lin had taken the following random notes, in 1963 in his Work Handbook, which were considered similarly incriminating:

Patience, the scientific foundation of forebearance. . . . How can one spoil his great business of a lifetime for such a small man and such a small matter?[58]

These words were traced to a passage in the Confucian *Analects:* "Want of forebearance in small matters confounds great plans."[59] On another occasion Lin had said, "Those who do not lie will collapse. One cannot accomplish great things without telling lies."[60] Mencius said, "The great man does not think beforehand of his words whether they may be sincere, nor of actions whether they may be resolute . . ."[61] Further, in "An outline of 'Project 571' " had been the expression, "Success or death for virtue,"[62] a phrase reminding people of a Confucian saying:

> The determined scholar and the man of virtue will not seek to live at the expense of injuring their virtue. They will even sacrifice their lives to preserve their virtue complete.[63]

Seventh, Lin had not approved of the reeducation of cadres advocated by Mao, saying, "Cadres working in various organizations have been laid off; going to a May 7th Cadre School equals a disguised form of unemployment";[64] this echoed Mencius, who said:

> Those who labor with their minds govern others; those who labor with their strength are governed by others. Those who are governed by others support them; those who govern others are supported by them. This is a principle universally recognized.[65]

Finally, Lin was charged with having indoctrinated his children with the tenets of Confucianism in the hope of creating a Lin dynasty. Lin had written a scroll for his son containing the following words: "Learn from the methodological spirit of having torn the dressed leather bindings twice";[66] this had been taken from words in the *Shih Chi:* "Confucius . . . studies the I Ching and the dressed leather bindings of it had been worn out twice."[67] And in a scroll for his daughter, Tou-tou, Lin had quoted exactly the words of Confucius: "The superior man is satisfied and composed; the mean man is always full of distress."[68]

These charges, even if true, seem contrived and tenuous; nevertheless, they are meant to be taken seriously as proof of Lin's guilt. Despite the determined efforts on the part of the leftists, the anti-Confucius and anti-Lin campaigns began to wind down in late 1974. In the meantime, Chou's public appearances also declined dramatically, for he claimed to be "getting old" and "in poor health." The accuracy of Chou's statement was confirmed by Senator Henry Jackson who visited Chou in a Peking hospital, and by official Chinese reports that Chou had suffered a heart attack.[69]

Chou might have hoped to groom a successor as quickly and efficiently as possible because of his failing health. For this reason, Teng Hsiao-p'ing was not only returned to public life, but also given, whenever possible, the responsibilities and exposure usually accorded a premier. For example, he acted on Chou's behalf at official functions honoring the visiting former president of Cyprus, Archbishop Makarios,[70] and Britain's former Prime Minister Edward Heath.[71] This became more obvious when Teng came to the United Nations as a representative of the People's Republic in April 1974 and went to France in May 1975 to negotiate with the Common Market. It was indeed ironic that someone condemned earlier as the "number 2 person in authority taking the capitalist road" could make such a quick and complete comeback; yet all available evidence indicated that he had assumed the number 3 position.

## NOTES

1. *Chung-hua yueh-pao (China Monthly)*, no. 697 (October 1, 1973), p. 17.

2. For a description of the difference between a plenum and a "central work conference," see Parris H. Chang, "Research Notes on the Changing Loci of Decision in the Chinese Communist Party," *The China Quarterly*, no. 44 (October/December 1970), pp. 169–81.

3. *Peking Review*, nos. 35 and 36 (September 7, 1973), p. 29.

4. The official agenda included a political report by Chou En-lai, a report on the revision of the Party Constitution by Wang Hung-wen, and the election of a new CC, as noted in Ibid., p. 5.

5. See, for example, Henry S. Bradsher, "China: The Radical Offensive," *Asian Survey*, November 1973, p. 997.

6. *Peking Review*, nos. 35 and 36 (September 7, 1973), p. 17.

7. Ibid.

8. Ibid., p. 19.

9. Ibid., p. 7.

10. *Peking Review*, no. 1 (January 7, 1972), p. 11.

11. According to *Studies on Chinese Communism*, no. 9 (September 1973), p. 30, Wang Pai-tan, a regular of the Ninth CC, changed his name to Wang Pai-teh, probably because his original name sounds like a Chinese curse word and thus too undignified for a member of the CC. Wang was reelected as an alternate to the Tenth CC. This being so, there should be 58 alternates in the Tenth CC who were not members of the Ninth CC, rather than 59, as reported by *The China Quarterly*, no. 56 (October/December 1973), p. 805. The other two regulars demoted to alternate status were Shen Mou-kung and Yang Fu-chen.

12. *China News Analysis*, no. 932 (September 7, 1973), p. 4.

13. *Studies on Chinese Communism 8*, no. 4 (April 1974), p. 71.

14. For a more thorough discussion on Wang, see Parris H. Chang, "Political Profiles: Wang Hung-wen and Li Teh-sheng," *The China Quarterly*, no. 57 (January/March 1974), pp. 124–28.

15. *Studies on Chinese Communism 7*, no. 1 (January 1973), p. 9.

16. *Studies on Chinese Communism 7*, no. 9 (September 1973), p. 29.

17. Institute for the Study of Chinese Communist Problems, *Important CCP Documents of the Great Proletarian Cultural Revolution* (Taipei: Institute for the Study of Chinese Communist Problems, 1973), p. 157.

18. Ibid., p. 315.

19. Ibid., pp. 261, 264.

20. Ibid., p. 153.

21. *Fei-ch'ing yueh-pao (Chinese Communist Affairs Monthly) 16,* no. 8 (October 1973), p. 13.

22. "China '73 Focus," *Far Eastern Economic Review, 59* no. 39 (October 1, 1973), p. 5.

23. Donald W. Klein and Lois B. Hager, "The Ninth Central Committee," *The China Quarterly,* no. 45 (January/March 1971), p. 51.

24. See Richard Wich, "The Tenth Party Congress: The Power Structure and the Succession Question," *The China Quarterly,* no. 58 (April/June 1974), p. 237.

25. *Peking Review,* nos. 35 and 36 (September 7, 1973), p. 32.

26. Ibid.

27. Ibid., p. 27.

28. *China Monthly,* no. 697 (October 1, 1973), p. 52.

29. Ellis Joffe, "The Chinese Army After the Cultural Revolution: The Effects of Intervention," *The China Quarterly,* no. 55 (July/September 1973), p. 458.

30. *Studies on Chinese Communism 8,* no. 1 (January 1974), p. 20.

31. See Peter R. Moody, Jr., "The New Anti-Confucian Campaign in China: The First Round," *Asian Survey 14,* April 1974, pp. 307–24.

32. *Far Eastern Economic Review 60,* no. 18 (May 6, 1974), p. 28.

33. James Legge, *The Chinese Classics,* 5 volumes. (Hong Kong: Hong Kong University Press, 1960), Vol. 2: *The Works of Mencius,* p. 250.

34. *People's Daily,* February 2, 1974.

35. *Peking Review,* no. 6 (February 8, 1974), p. 5.

36. *Red Flag,* no. 3 (1974), cited in *Survey of the People's Republic of China Press,* no. 74–13 (March 25–29, 1974), p. 82.

37. *Issues and Studies 11,* no. 4 (April 1975), p. 94.

38. Ibid., p. 95.

39. James Legge, *The Chinese Classics,* vol. 1, *The Confucian Analects* (Hong Kong: Hong Kong University Press, 1960), pp. 263–64.

40. *Issues and Studies 11,* no. 4 (April 1975), p. 96.

41. Legge, vol. 2, *The Works of Mencius,* p. 232.

42. *Issues and Studies 11,* no. 4 (April 1975), p. 96.

43. Legge, vol. 1, p. 202.

44. *Issues and Studies 11,* no. 4 (April 1975), p. 97.

45. Ibid., p. 99.

46. Legge, vol. 2, pp. 313–14.

47. Ibid., p. 232.

48. Ibid., p. 244.

49. *Issues and Studies 11,* no. 4 (April 1975), p. 101.

50. Ibid.

51. Legge, vol. 1, p. 211.

52. *Issues and Studies 11,* no. 4 (April 1975), p. 102.

53. Ibid.

54. Ibid., p. 103.

55. Legge, vol. 2, pp. 196–97.

56. Legge, vol. 1, pp. 193–94.

57. *Issues and Studies 11,* no. 4 (April 1975), p. 105.

58. Ibid., p. 108.

59. Legge, vol. 1, p. 302.

60. *Issues and Studies 11,* no. 4 (April 1975), p. 109.

61. Legge, vol. 2, pp. 321–22.

62. *Issues and Studies 11,* no. 4 (April 1975), p. 110.

63. Legge, vol. 1, p. 297.

64. *Issues and Studies 11,* no. 4 (April 1975), p. 110.
65. Legge, vol. 2, pp. 249–50.
66. *Issues and Studies 11,* no. 4 (April 1975), p. 114.
67. Ibid.
68. Legge, vol. 1, p. 207.
69. *New York Times,* July 15, 1974.
70. *New York Times,* May 18, 1974.
71. *New York Times,* May 25, 1974.

CHAPTER

# 8

## THE FOURTH
## NATIONAL PEOPLE'S CONGRESS:
## RESTRUCTURING THE
## NATIONAL GOVERNMENT

To provide a semblance of legitimacy and signal a return to complete normalcy, the National People's Congress (NPC), regarded as the "only legislative authority in the country,"[1] had to be convened as soon as possible. The Constitution of the People's Republic of China, originally adopted by the First National People's Congress in 1954, had to be revised to take into consideration the many unprecedented changes brought about by the Great Proletarian Cultural Revolution, including the dismissal of a chief of state (Liu Shao-ch'i) and the creation of RCs. Furthermore, the NPC, according to the constitution, was "elected for a term of four years"[2] and should meet "once a year";[3] the Third NPC had last met in 1965. Therefore, the Fourth NPC was long overdue.

The Chinese Communist leadership was not unaware of this problem. As early as September 1967, Mao, in a speech entitled "Great Strategic Deployment," had said, "The Party Congress should be convened, so should the People's Congress. I think it can take place around this time next year."[4] Then on November 27, 1967, the CC, in conjunction with the CCRG, announced in a notice soliciting opinions regarding the Ninth Party Congress:

> The majority of our comrades proposed that the Ninth Party Congress should be convened before National Day next fall. The National People's Congress should be held after the Ninth Party Congress in order to dismiss Liu Shao-ch'i so that all those who would appear on T'ien An Men [Square] next year will be the leaders of a new Party and country under Mao's proletarian headquarters.[5]

After the Ninth Party Congress in April 1969, plans to convene the Fourth NPC were actively undertaken. In July of 1970 a special committee was established to draft a revised constitution, with Mao Tse-tung and Lin Piao as its chairman and vice-chairman, respectively.[6] This draft (hereafter, the first draft) was "basically approved"[7] by the Second Plenum of the Ninth CC, which also announced in a September 6, 1970, communique that the people's congress would be held at a "suitable time," a promise repeated in the joint 1971 New Year's Day editorial by *People's Daily, Red Flag,* and *Liberation Army Daily:*

> We are going to greet the 50th anniversary of the great, glorious and correct Communist Party of China and the Fourth National People's Congress.[8]

However, before the congress could materialize, the purge of Lin Piao took place, plunging the country once again into a period of great uncertainty until the Tenth Party Congress met in August 1973. In his report to this congress, Chou En-lai reassured the delegates, "We shall soon convene the Fourth National People's Congress."[9]

For a while, there were signs that the Fourth NPC was indeed imminent. According to a Hong Kong source, delegates to the congress were elected in October 1973,[10] and on November 12, 1973, the First Plenum of the Tenth CC adopted a revised version of the first draft (hereafter, the second draft) of the constitution.[11] The joint editorial on January 1, 1974, reiterated the earlier message that "we should make outstanding achievements in all fields of work to greet the Fourth National People's Congress."[12]

During 1974, more information became available indicating that the convocation of this long-overdue congress was not far away. On March 10, a vice-chairwoman of the Szechwan RC, Tan K'un-yung, said in a radio broadcast that she was "elected not long ago by the masses to serve as a delegate for the soon-to-be-convened Fourth People's Congress";[13] and Teng Hsiaop'ing, while acting in his capacity as vice-premier, informed visiting Japanese delegations in both May and October 1974, "The Fourth NPC is now under active preparation and we hope to convene it as soon as possible."[14] To another group of Japanese visitors on December 5, Teng repeated again, "Delegates to the NPC have been elected and hopefully, it will convene within this year."[15]

Yet despite these repeated assurances, it seemed the congress would never take place, and the 1975 joint New Year's Day editorial failed to make any mention of it whatsoever. Therefore it came as a surprise when the *New China News Agency* reported on January 18, 1975, that the Fourth NPC had in fact met in Peking from January 13 to 17, 1975.

The Fourth NPC, like the Ninth and Tenth Party Congresses, was shrouded in secrecy. All past sessions of the NPCs had been widely publicized, and during the First NPC, comments made by its delegates were reported in *People's Daily.* Also notable was the brevity of the Fourth NPC, since, excluding the preparatory meeting held from January 5 to 11, 1975, it convened for only five days, and was thus the shortest on record.* The actual working time was even less. The first day was taken up by Chou En-lai's report on "The Work of the Government."[16] and Chang Ch'un-ch'iao's report on "The Revision of the Constitution,"[17] and the last day was allotted to voting, with only three days (including a half-day devoted to the funeral service of Li Fu-ch'un) for discussion of the constitutional revisions and the appointment of a State Council. Under these circumstances, it is unlikely that the 2,864 delegates in attendance, of the 2,885 elected, did more than rubber-stamp what was submitted to them for approval.

The newly adopted constitution is indeed a cursory, skimpy document with 30 articles in less than 4,200 Chinese characters, in contrast to its predecessor, which contained 106 articles in 14,000 words. While many substantive issues have been completely disregarded and meticulous detail replaced by vague statements of principles, a careful comparison of the two documents, nevertheless, reveals significant changes affecting many aspects of Chinese political life.

## THE ELIMINATION OF THE POSITION OF STATE CHAIRMAN

The 1954 State Constitution had made provision for the position of chairman of the People's Republic, whose election, powers, and responsibilities were clearly specified;[18] and not unexpectedly, Mao Tse-tung, in addition to holding the chairmanship of the CCP, was simultaneously elected by the First NPC as state chairman. However, disheartened by the failure of the Three Red Banners plan (discussed earlier) and confronted with growing internal opposition within the CCP hierarchy, Mao had asked to be relieved of his state post at the Sixth Plenum of the Eighth CC in December 1968, claiming later:

My intention then was to build up the prestige of others so that when I went to see the Lord there would be no terrific shock in the country.[19]

As discussed earlier, Liu Shao-ch'i had replaced Mao as state chairman in 1959 but was subsequently expelled from "all posts both inside and outside the Party"[20] at the Ninth Party Congress in April 1969, and Lin Piao had aspired to succeed Mao as state chairman until his death in 1971.

The first draft of the 1975 state constitution, adopted (in 1970) when Lin

---

*Previously, the two shortest sessions, both 11 days, had been the Fifth Plenum of the First NPC, which had met from February 1 to 11, 1958, and the First Plenum of the Second NPC, which had convened from April 18 to 28, 1959. The Second Plenum of the First NPC had been the longest on record, meeting for 26 days, from July 5 to 30, 1955.

was still in power, had not specifically mentioned the position of state chairman but declared Mao

the great leader of the people of all nationalities of the whole country, the head of the proletariat of our country, supreme commander of all armed forces of the whole country.[21]

Lin was described as "Chairman Mao's close comrade-in-arms and successor, deputy commander of all armed forces of the whole country."[22] When the second draft was adopted in 1973, after the purge of Lin, Mao's role remained the same, but the portion pertaining to Lin was naturally discarded. The 1975 constitution did not even mention Mao by name; it said only that "Marxism-Leninism-Mao Tse-tung Thought is the theoretical basis guiding the thinking of our nation,"[23] and assigned the ceremonial and routine duties of the state chairman, such as "receiving foreign diplomatic envoys" and "ratifying and denouncing treaties concluded with foreign states"[24] to the chairman of the Standing Committee of the National People's Congress—Chu Teh (elected in 1959 when Liu Shao-ch'i had become the state chairman).

## CONTINUED REASSERTION OF PARTY SUPREMACY

In doing away with the state chairman, the 1975 Constitution assigned his responsibilities as commander of the nation's armed forces to the chairman of the CC of the CCP.[25] While one can interpret this move as an enhancement of Mao's personal power, an equally valid interpretation must be the consolidation of Party control over the military. That this policy had already been implemented at local levels had been confirmed by radio broadcasts in December 1974 from Shantung, Hupei, Fukien, Liaoning, and Szechwan provinces, relaying the order:

Field Armies should accept the leadership of the Provincial Party Committees in carrying out assignments related to the localities where they are stationed. All military cadres, while participating in the work of local areas, should accept the unified leadership of the local Party committees.[26]

The relationship between the CCP and the NPC also has changed in a substantive way. The Communist Party is now "the core of leadership of the whole Chinese people,"[27] through which "the working class exercises leadership over the state."[28] The National People's Congress, though still the "highest organ of state power,"[29] now must function "under the leadership of the Communist Party of China."[30] According to the 1954 Constitution, the NPC had the power "to decide on the choice of the premier of the State Council upon recommendation by the Chairman of the PRC, and of the component members of the State Council upon recommendation by the premier."[31] Though still authorized to make such appointments or removals, the NPC must now act "on the proposal of the Central Committee of the Communist Party of China."[32]

The role of other political parties in China today is obscure, since they are not mentioned in the 1975 Constitution. The Chinese People's Political Consultative Conference (CPPCC), the organizational form of the people's democratic united front,[33] which had in a broad past legitimized the participation of non-Communist parties, now failed to follow its past practice of meeting at about the same time as the NPC but instead sponsored a conference shortly after the conclusion of the Fourth NPC to commemorate the "Taiwan February 28 Incident,"[34] an indication that it still exists. Furthermore, there are presently 4 vice-chairmen of the NPC, of a total of 22, who are not members of the Communist party: Sung Ch'ing-ling, Ngapo Ngawang Jigme, Hu Chueh-wen, and Hsu Teh-yen.

## A REDUCTION IN THE POWER AND STATURE OF THE STATE COUNCIL

The State Council, described in the 1954 Constitution as "the executive organ of the highest state authority" and "the highest administrative organ of the state,"[35] had been expanded at the Third NPC in 1965 to 40 ministries, 9 commissions, 7 general offices, and 24 directly subordinate offices (*chih-shu chi-kou*), but has now been reduced to 26 ministries and 3 commissions in order to comply with the 1975 stipulation that "[e]very organ of state must apply the principle of efficient and simple administration."[36] More significant than this cut in size is the decline in the State Council's power and stature reflected by the failure of the 1975 constitution to enumerate the powers which in the past had fallen within its jurisdiction. Though still authorized to "formulate administrative measures and issue decisions and orders,"[37] the State Council no longer "verif[ies] their execution."[38] Also disappearing from the new constitution were the State Council's power to "submit bills to the NPC or its Standing Committee";[39] to "revise or annul inappropriate orders and directives issued by Ministers and Heads of Commissions"[40] or "decisions and orders issued by local administrative organs of state";[41] to "guide the building up of the defense forces"[42] (thus diluting the powers of the Ministry of Defense in the State Council); and to "ratify the status and boundaries of autonomous *chou,* counties, autonomous counties, and municipalities."[43] Omitted also is the power of the State Council to "appoint or remove administrative personnel according to provisions of law."[44] As noted earlier, the CC of the CCP, rather than the premier,[45] now makes the recommendations to the NPC regarding members of the State Council.[46]

## CHANGES IN THE NATURE OF THE STATE AND ECONOMIC SYSTEM

When the Chinese Communists had first come to power, they assumed a deceptively moderate posture in order to maximize support from all segments of the population, thereby better insuring a more orderly transition. Thus the Common Programme, which served as a temporary constitution from 1949 to 1954, had declared:

The Chinese People's Democratic Dictatorship is the state power of the people's democratic united front composed of the Chinese working class, peasantry, petty bourgeoisie, national bourgeoisie and other patriotic democratic elements, based on the alliance of workers and peasants and led by the working class.[47]

When the first constitution was adopted in 1954, the Peking regime had sufficiently consolidated its rule and begun to suppress gradually all opposition. Thus the 1954 constitution, though supposedly "an advance" from the Common Programme, eliminated the petty and national bourgeoisies from political participation; and the democratic united front was now to be "led by the Communist Party of China,"[48] rather than by the working class.

The 1975 Constitution has gone one step further, first by proclaiming Communist China a "socialist state of the dictatorship of the proletariat,"[49] rather than "a people's democratic state,"[50] and secondly, by eliminating two of the four types of "ownership of means of production" permitted earlier—"capitalist ownership" and "ownership by individual working people"[51]—and retaining only "socialist ownership by the whole people and socialist collective ownership by working people."[52]

## THE ABANDONMENT OF THE ELECTION SYSTEM

One striking characteristic of the 1954 Constitution had been its minutely detailed provisions covering all aspects of the state's election procedure. It stated that delegates "to the people's congresses of provinces, municipalities directly under the central authority, counties, and municipalities divided into districts are elected by the people's congresses of the next lower level"[53] indirectly and "by secret ballots,"[54] and delegates to "the people's congresses of municipalities not divided into districts, municipal districts, *hsiang,* nationality *hsiang* and towns are directly elected by the voters"[55] through "a show of hands."[56]

In reality, however, the elections were by no means free. Voters usually had no choice: in the 1964 election for delegates to the Third NPC from Peking, exactly 101 candidates ran for 101 positions.[57] Furthermore, the CCP could exert its influence more indirectly by deciding upon a list of candidates with other groups before submitting it to the NPC. Nevertheless, there was at least the facade of going through the motions "from the bottom up," with initiatives coming basically from the lower levels. The 1975 constitution modified this system by introducing the phrase "through democratic consultation."[58] In practice this entails negotiation and bargaining among competing groups and requires prior approval of the CCP, thus reversing the electoral process to flow "from the top down."

In the past, the number of delegates to an NPC has been determined by the size of the population. According to the "Resolution Regarding the Number and Election of Delegates to the NPC," adopted by the Fourth Plenum of the Second NPC on December 3, 1963:

> One delegate should be elected for every 400,000 in the provinces and autonomous regions with a minimum of 10 delegates, no matter how small the population, and for every 50,000 in the centrally-directed cities with a population in excess of 300,000. Three hundred delegates should be allotted to the national minorities; 120 to the armed forces and 30 to overseas Chinese.[59]

Yet for some unexplained reason, there has been a reduction of 155 delegates; 3,400 attended the Third NPC, but only 2,885 were elected to the Fourth Congress, despite an acknowledged population increase from 1963 to 1975 (exact statistics are not known). In addition, overseas Chinese as a group are no longer entitled to representation in the NPC.[60]

## Revolutionary Committees as One of the "New-Born Things"

Originally conceived as a "temporary organ of power," the RCs have now been declared one of the "new-born things"[61] of the Cultural Revolution. As "permanent organs of the local people's congresses"[62] with legislative powers, RCs are "at the same time the local people's government,"[63] assuming the executive and administrative functions of the people's councils that had existed before the Cultural Revolution. The "three-in-one combination," which referred to the earlier coalition of military, revolutionary cadres, and mass representatives, has been officially modified to mean the alliance of "the old, the middle-aged and the young."[64] Normally, local people's congresses are convened after the NPC to determine members of the people's councils, or RCs in the present case, but there is little information available indicating that they are forthcoming.

## Downgrading the Judiciary

The 1975 Constitution has undermined the independence of the judiciary by eliminating the Supreme People's Procuratorate at the national level, which, according to the 1954 Constitution,

> exercises procuratorial authority over all departments of the State Council, all local organs of state, persons working in organs of state, and citizens, to ensure observance of the law.[65]

The people's procuratorates at the local level, which were regarded as "independent" and "not subject to interference by local organs of state,"[66] and performed similar procuratorial functions at their respective levels, have also been omitted from the new constitution. Furthermore, it is worth noting that judges of the people's courts are no longer elected by the people's congresses,[67] but are now appointed or removed by the RCs.[68] The 1975 Constitution stipulates that the people's courts must be "responsible and accountable" not only to the people's congresses, but also to "their permanent organs."[69] Thus the RCs have acquired a judicial authority in addition to their executive and legislative prerogatives. The rudimentary separation of powers provided by the 1954 constitution has now been officially discarded.

## Curtailment of Citizens' Rights

Many of the citizens' rights previously guaranteed are not mentioned in the present constitution. These include the right of peasants "to own land";[70] of "handicraftsmen and other non-agricultural individual working people to own means of production";[71] of "capitalists to own means of production and other capital."[72] No longer does "[t]he state protect the right of citizens to inherit private property according to law."[73] In the past, citizens could not be arrested except by a decision of a people's court or with the approval of a people's procuratorate;[74] now arrests can be made "with the sanction of a public security organ,"[75] as well as by the decision of a people's court. Even more alarming is that the right of the accused to a defense[76] also has been ignored in the present constitution.

Reportedly as a result of Mao Tse-tung's personal recommendation, the freedom to strike becomes a new addition to the list of freedoms guaranteed, though in reality these promises have seldom been honored. The 1975 Constitution no longer mentions the "freedom of residence and freedom to change [their] residence,"[77] an apparent attempt to legitimize the *hsia-fang* policy, thereby preventing the return to the cities of the more than 60 million young people[78] who had been sent to the countryside as one solution to the problem of controlling urban overpopulation while at the same time augmenting the agricultural labor force. Because of unaccustomed hardships in the rural villages, ill-treatment by farmers who resent these "extra mouths to feed," and the exploitative attitudes of Party cadres,[79] a large number deserted their assignments, especially during the turmoil of the Cultural Revolution, and returned to their urban homes[80] where they now live "underground" because they lack residence registration[81] and food rations. The Communist government has been urging them to "immediately return to their own units."[82]

Finally, the old constitution required the people of China to "abide by the Constitution and the law, uphold discipline at work, keep public order and respect social ethics."[83] To these, the new constitution has added the obligation to support "the leadership of the Communist Party of China" and the "socialist system."[84]

Unlike its predecessor, the 1975 Constitution gives the impression of being superficially and ambiguously framed, possibly due to a continued absence of a consensus within the Chinese Communist leadership. The impact of the new constitution in real terms may be minimal, since most probably it will be ignored in times of emergency in a way similar to that in which the 1954 Constitution was so frequently and conveniently overlooked at the height of the Cultural Revolution.

## New Factional Alignments

The struggle for power among the competing factions continued in the selection of NPC leadership and the State Council. According to a Hong Kong source,[85] there were plans to install Chiang Ch'ing as chairman of the Standing Committee of the NPC, evidenced by the substitution of the word "director" for "chairman," because otherwise, Chiang's official designation would have sounded, in Chinese, too much like Chiang Kai-shek's official title during World War II.* Chu Teh was reelected chairman, however, and no change was made.

---

*If *chu-jen* (director) were not substituted for *wei-yüan-ch'ang* (chairman), then Chiang Ch'ing would be addressed as Chiang *wei-yüan-ch'ang,* which in Chinese sounds very similar to Chiang Kai-shek's official title during World War II.

Of the 18 vice-chairmen of the Third People's Congress, 8 were reelected (K'ang Sheng, Liu Po-ch'eng, Kuo Mo-jo, Hsü Hsiang-ch'ien, Li Ching-ch'üan, Saifudin, Ngapo Ngawang-Jigme, and Chou Chien-jen); 6 died (Ho Hsiang-ning, Huang Yen-p'ei, Ch'en Chu-tung, Yang Ming-hen, Chen Chien, and Chang Chih-chung); and 4 were purged (P'eng Chen, Liu Feng, Liu Ning-yi, and Li Hsueh-feng). Now there were 22 vice-chairmen, including Tung Pi-wu, who died in April 1975, and Sung Ch'ing-ling, both former vice-chairmen of the NPC. Further, 18 (77.8 percent) of the 22 vice-chairmen are either senior cadres (15) or military men (3); only 4 (22.2 percent) can be linked with the CCRG leftist faction: K'ang Sheng, Wu Teh, Li Su-wen, and Yao Lien-wei. K'ang is now in poor health. Wu is a Politburo member and concurrently chairman of the Peking RC and first political commissar of the Peking MR. Li and Yao have had little experience in politics; the former was a salesman in a Shenyang department store, and the latter, a vice-chairman of the Shensi Trade Union.

The Standing Committee of the National People's Congress increased by 50 percent, or from 96 to 144 members; 28 (29.2 percent) were reelected, constituting 19.2 percent of the present enlarged membership. Another 19.2 percent are liberated cadres, military leaders, and leaders from educational and scientific circles. The most significant group, 87 members (61.6 percent), are relatively young mass representatives who are sympathetic to, if not actually aligned with, the leftists. Most of them have risen to prominence since the Cultural Revolution after having acquired leadership positions at the provincial level and below; 22 were elected as regular or alternate members of the CC (12 are regulars and 10 are alternates).

The Fourth NPC "elected by secret ballot" the premier and other members of the State Council on the basis of lists of nominees put forward by "the Second Plenum of the Tenth CC."[86] Yet, it was rumored, the Politburo did not agree with the final results.[87] Chou En-lai retained the premiership, but the State Council that emerged from the Cultural Revolution is a vastly different organization in terms of the number and composition of its personnel. The number of vice-premiers has been reduced from 16 to 12; 2, Li Hsien-nien and Teng Hsiao-p'ing, were reappointed; and only 3 of the 29 ministers had held the same position previously.

Teng Hsiao-p'ing's appointment as first vice-premier, thus legally designated to succeed Chou in the event of the latter's death or incapacity, was of greater importance than Chou's reappointment as premier. An additional 5 vice-premiers who showed "pragmatic" tendencies in the past could be expected to follow the lead of Chou and Teng: Li Hsien-nien, for many years Chou's major assistant in financial matters; Ch'en Hsi-lien, commander of the Peking MR and one of Chou's trusted generals; Ku Mu, an experienced cadre in the field of state planning and, like Teng, purged during the Cultural Revolution but later liberated; Yu Ch'iu-li, also a liberated veteran official in the State Council; and Wang Chen, a military man once closely connected with Ho Lung.

The leftists can also claim six vice-premiers. Chang Ch'un-ch'iao was appointed second vice-premier, placing him second in line of succession to Chou. Chi Teng-k'uei, a Politburo member, was removed to make room for Li Teh-sheng, enabling Teng Hsiao-p'ing to assume Li's position as vice-chairman of the CCP. Chi remains, however, the political commissar of the Peking MR and a vice-chairman of the Honan RC and secretary of its party committee. Sun Chien, reported to be a naval officer,[88] is an unknown figure who first appeared on the national scene when he was elected an alternate member of the Tenth CC. Ch'en Yung kuei and Wu Kuei-hsien are typical mass representatives. Ch'en, a "model peasant" of the well-publicized Tachai Commune in Hsiyang, Shansi, was formerly the chairman of its Tachai Production Brigade RC, and Wu, a woman, was a "model worker" in a cotton mill in Sian, Shensi. Both rose rapidly during the Cultural Revolution and were promoted to regular and alternate member, respectively, of the Politburo of the Tenth CC. Comparatively new to politics, they probably play only a symbolic or window-dressing role. The last vice-premier identified with the CCRG is Hua Kuo-feng, who had become prominent nationally during the Cultural Revolution and served first as secretary of the Party committee in Mao's home town—Hsiangtan, Hunan—before being promoted to first secretary of the Hunan PPC during the Cultural Revolution. Summoned later to Peking, he became one of the pillars of the CCRG and was elected to the Politburo of the Tenth CC.

But 24 (80.3 percent) of the 29 ministers exercising actual control over the daily operations of the central government can be categorized as having been loosely allied with Chou. (Of these, 16 are senior cadres and 8 are military men.) Ch'iao Kuan-hua, a longtime intimate of Chou and former liaison representative in the United States, has been promoted to minister of foreign affairs. Yeh Chien-ying, on whom Chou had relied heavily to run the national military establishment since the purge of Lin Piao, has been appointed minister of national defense, a post he has held in an acting capacity. Probably because of his advanced age, Yeh does not hold a vice-premiership in the State Council, which past defense ministers usually assumed. Another appointment deserving notice is that of Chou Jung-hsin. A liberated cadre once close to Chou En-lai, Chou Jung-hsin now heads the Ministry of Education, the subject of a vicious attack during the Cultural Revolution and, for a while, dominated by the CCRG.[89]

The leftists can claim only 5 (19.7 percent) ministerial appointments. Vice-premier Hua Kuo-feng also holds the position of minister of public security, a ministry whose powers and jurisdiction have been newly enlarged. In this post, Hua easily counterbalances Yeh Chien-ying. Liu Hsi-yao, a veteran cadre favored by Chiang Ch'ing after the Cultural Revolution, was assigned the directorship of the Science and Education Group of the State Council. As minister of the Second Machine Building, he is in charge of nuclear development in China. The Ministry of Culture, deeply embroiled in the turmoil of the Cultural Revolution,[90] has understandably fallen into the hands of the leftists and is headed by Yu Hui-yung, a musician who had joined the CCRG during the Cultural Revolution. He formerly served as vice-director of the Cultural Group in the State Council. The other two ministers identified with the leftist group occupy posts of minor importance: Liu Hsiang-p'ing, the wife of Hsieh Fu-chih, is now the minister of public health; and Chuang Tse-tung, a world's champion ping-pong player, was promoted from vice-chairman to chairman of the Physical, Cultural and Sports Commission.

The allocation of State Council appointments in the Fourth NPC reflected the spirit of compromise between the leftists and those rallying around Chou En-lai who had shared a moderate view. On one hand, some very prominent members of the CCRG who, as elected members of the NPC Presidium made preparations for the congress and probably attended it, were unable to obtain any additional positions of substance; this group would include Chiang Ch'ing, Yao Wen-yuan, and Wang Hung-wen. Several others, however, such as Chang Ch'un-ch'iao and Hua Kuo-feng, did manage to penetrate the State Council, the bastion of Chou En-lai traditionally dominated by moderate bureaucrats. At the same time none of Chou's prominent associates lost his position.

With the adoption of a new state constitution and the reorganization of the central governmental apparatus, China can claim a nominally complete return to normalcy, yet what the future holds is far more complicated and unsettling. In the same issue publicizing the state constitution, *Red Flag,* which, like the *People's Daily,* has been controlled by the leftists since the early days of the Cultural Revolution, published three articles that seemed to be out of tune with the occasion. The first article, "Conscientiously Study the Theory of the Dictatorship of the Proletariat," pointed out that "the class struggle is by no means over," and cautioned:

> Only by seriously studying this theory can we deepen our criticism of such sinister wares as fixing farm output quotas for individual households with each on its own, material incentives and economism advocated by Liu Shao-ch'i and Lin Piao; only thus can we deepen our criticism of capitalist tendencies, such as erroneous ideas and styles of work as servility to things foreign, the doctrine of trailing behind [other countries] at a snail's pace and extravagance and waste so as to promote the development of socialist revolution on the economic front.[91]

"Historical Tasks of the Dictatorship of the Proletariat," the second article, warned:

> Not reconciled to their extinction, the overthrown exploiting classes inevita-

bly turn their hope for restoration into attempts at restoration. With fury grown tenfold and hatred grown a hundredfold, they carry out a desperate struggle against the proletariat in a vain attempt to recapture their lost power and ruling position. In addition to taking the field themselves, they pay special attention to recruiting agents from within the Party of the proletariat, and through their agents, they try to change the Party's line, practice revisionism, engage in splittist activities and intrigues and conspiracies so as to achieve their criminal aim of subverting the dictatorship of the proletariat and restoring capitalism.[92]

The third article, "Uphold the Dictatorship of the Proletariat over the Bourgeoisie," further pointed out:

> Now, Liu Shao-ch'i and Lin Piao have already been overthrown; but, the class foundation to engender revisionism still exists. The struggle to topple or consolidate the dictatorship of the proletariat has not yet finished, the struggle to oppose and prevent revisionism has not yet finished.[93]

On February 9, 1975, *People's Daily* joined the discussion by publishing an article, "Study Well the Dictatorship of the Proletariat." It began by quoting Mao's "recent," "important" instruction:

> Why did Lenin speak of exercising dictatorship over the bourgeoisie? This question must be thoroughly understood. 'Lack of clarity on this question will lead to revisionism. This should be made known to the whole nation.' "[94]

Pointing out that "on this question, some of our comrades, too, have got muddled ideas of one kind or another, and even regard certain capitalist stuff as socialist," the article emphasized:

> the attitude towards the dictatorship of the proletariat is the touchstone that distinguishes genuine Marxism from sham Marxism. All revisionists invariably try by hook or crook to distort, attack and liquidate the dictatorship of the proletariat.[95]

The issue of revisionism was a serious enough matter to warrant two more articles written by major leftists, Yao Wen-yuan and Chang Ch'un-ch'iao, in the following issues of *Red Flag*. Yao Wen-yuan, quoting Mao, discussed the remaining problems in the present economic system:

> China is a socialist country. Before liberation, she was more or less like capitalism. Even now she practices an eight-grade wage system, distribution to each according to his work, and exchange by means of money, which are

scarcely different from those in the old society. What is different is that the
system of ownership has changed.[96]

In addition, Yao pointed out, there are inequities which should be corrected
such as those between workers and peasants, town and country, and finally,
between manual and mental labor.

In his article, "On Exercising All-Round Dictatorship Over the Bourgeoisie," Chang Ch'un-ch'iao wrote that "there is still the danger for China to turn
revisionist" because "the old landlords and capitalists, unreconciled to their
defeat, are still there" and "old ideas and the force of habit are trying obsti-
nately to hold back the growth of socialist new things."[97] Chang even cited
statistics to argue that "private ownership still exists in parts of industry,
agriculture, as well as commerce," and that "socialist public ownership" still
includes two kinds. As long as "collective ownership," in addition to "ownership by the whole people," is allowed in China, Chang regarded the goal of
a socialist society, advocated by Marx and Lenin, to eliminate private ownership and convert all means of production into the common possession of
everyone, as not yet accomplished. According to Chang, since "new bourgeois
elements are, as Lenin put it, being engendered daily and hourly," "the emergence of new bourgeois elements," unless restricted, is "likewise inevitable"
and will even "grow faster." Concluding on an omnious note, he said, "On no
account should we relax our vigilance," and "neither in theory nor in practice
should we overlook the very arduous tasks that lie ahead."[98]

That such a quick succession of repetitious pronouncements were devoted
to a single theme at a time when new compromises should have been worked
out seems to indicate that the leftists were not complacent about the results
of the Fourth NPC, and that the central issue of when and how to implement
communism in China remained unresolved.

## NOTES

1. 1954 State Constitution, hereafter 1954 Constitution, Article 22, cited in Albert B.
Blaustein, *Legal Documents of Communist China* (S. Hackensack, N.J.: Fred B. Rothman, 1962),
pp. 1–33.

2. Ibid., Article 24.

3. Ibid., Article 25.

4. Institute for the Study of Chinese Communist Problems, *Important CCP Documents of
the Great Proletarian Cultural Revolution* (hereafter cited as *Important CCP Documents*) (Taipei:
Institute for the Study of Chinese Communist Problems, 1973), p. 214.

5. Ibid., p. 13.

6. *Studies on Chinese Communism 9,* no. 2 (February 1975), pp. 42–43.

7. "Document of the Central Committee of the Chinese Communist Party" (*Chung-fa,* no.
56, 1970), cited in *The Lin Piao Affair: Power Politics and Military Coup,* ed. Michael Y. M. Kau
(White Plains, NY: International Arts and Sciences Press, 1975), pp. 106–9.

8. *People's Daily,* January 1, 1971.

9. Chou En-lai, "Report to the Tenth People's Congress," *Peking Review,* nos. 35 and 36 (September 7, 1973), p. 25.

10. *China Monthly,* no. 714 (March 1, 1975), p. 30.

11. "Revised Draft of the 'Constitution of the People's Republic of China' ", *Issues and Studies 10,* no. 14 (November 1974), pp. 109–13.

12. *People's Daily,* January 1, 1974.

13. *Studies on Chinese Communism 9,* no. 2 (February 1975), p. 43.

14. Ibid.

15. Ibid.

16. *Peking Review,* no. 4 (January 24, 1975), pp. 21–25.

17. Ibid., pp. 18–20.

18. 1954 Constitution, Articles 39–46.

19. *Red Line Edition (Hung hsien-pan),* December 19, 1966, cited in *Chinese Law and Government,* no. 1 (Spring 1968), p. 7.

20. Lin Piao, "Report to the Ninth National Congress of the Communist Party of China," *Peking Review,* no. 18 (April 30, 1969), p. 21.

21. "Revised Draft of the Constitution of the People's Republic of China" (September 6, 1970), *Issues and Studies 6,* no. 3 (December 1970), pp. 89–90.

22. Ibid., p. 90.

23. 1975 State Constitution (hereafter cited as 1975 Constitution), Article 2, cited in *Peking Review,* no. 4 (January 24, 1975), pp. 12–17.

24. 1975 Constitution, Article 18.

25. 1975 Constitution, Article 15.

26. *Chinese Communist Affairs Monthly 18,* no. 2 (April 1975), p. 61.

27. 1975 Constitution, Article 2.

28. Ibid.

29. 1975 Constitition, Article 16.

30. Ibid.

31. 1954 Constitution, Article 27.

32. 1975 Constitution, Article 17.

33. 1954 Constitution, Preamble.

34. *People's Daily,* March 1, 1975.

35. 1954 Constitution, Article 47.

36. 1975 Constitution, Article 11.

37. 1954 Constitution, Article 49 (1).

38. Ibid.; see 1975 Constitution, Article 20.

39. 1975 Constitution, Article 20 (2).

40. Ibid., (5).

41. Ibid., (6).

42. Ibid., (14).

43. Ibid., (15).

44. Ibid., (16).

45. 1975 Constitution, Article 17.

46. 1954 Constitution, Article 27.

47. Blaustein, Preamble, op. cit., p. 34.

48. 1954 Constitution, Preamble.

49. 1975 Constitution, Article 1.

50. 1954 Constitution, Article 1.

51. 1954 Constitution, Article 5.

52. 1975 Constitution, Article 5.

53. 1954 Constitution, Article 56.

54. Institute for the Study of Chinese Communist Problems *1967 Yearbook on Chinese Communism* (hereafter *1967 Yearbook*) (Taipei: Institute for the Study of Chinese Communist Problems, 1967), p. 412.

55. 1954 Constitution, Article 56.

56. *1967 Yearbook,* p. 412.

57. Ibid., p. 413.

58. 1975 Constitution, Article 3.

59. *1967 Yearbook,* op. cit., p. 414.

60. 1975 Constitution, Article 16.

61. *Red Flag,* no. 2 (1975), p. 21.

62. 1975 Constitution, Article 22.

63. Ibid.

64. 1975 Constitution, Article 11.

65. 1954 Constitution, Article 81.

66. 1954 Constitution, Article 83.

67. 1954 Constitution, Article 80.

68. 1975 Constitution, Article 25.

69. Ibid.

70. 1954 Constitution, Article 8.

71. 1954 Constitution, Article 9.

72. 1954 Constitution, Article 10.

73. 1954 Constitution, Article 12.

74. 1954 Constitution, Article 89.

75. 1975 Constitution, Article 28.

76. 1954 Constitution, Article 76.

77. 1954 Constitution, Article 90.

78. Institute for the Study of Chinese Communist Problems, *1974 Yearbook on Chinese Communism* (Taipei: Institute for the Study of Chinese Communist Problems, 1974), p. 2:206.

79. See, for example, the "Urgent Circular of the CCP Central Committee, the State Council, the Central Military Commission and the Central Cultural Revolution Group Concerning the Necessity for Educated Youths and Other Personnel Assigned to Work in Rural and Mountainous Areas to Persist in Staying in the Countryside to Grasp Revolution and Promote Production" (October 8, 1967), in Union Research Institute, *CCP Documents of the Great Proletarian Cultural Revolution* (hereafter cited as *CCP Documents*) (Hong Kong: Union Research Institute, 1969), p. 562.

80. See, for example, the "Circular of the CCP Central Committee Concerning the Opposition to Economism" (January 11, 1967), in *Important CCP Documents,* p. 89.

81. *CCP Documents,* p. 561.

82. See, for example, the "Circular of the CCP Central Committee and the State Council Concerning (Urban) Educated Youths Working in Rural and Mountainous Areas Who Go Out to Exchange Revolutionary Experience, Make Petitions, or Call on People at Higher Levels," ibid., p. 301.

83. 1954 Constitution, Article 100.

84. 1975 Constitution, Article 26.

85. *China Monthly,* no. 713 (February 1, 1975), p. 46.

86. *Peking Review,* no. 4 (January 24, 1975), p. 7.

87. *China Monthly,* no. 718 (July 1, 1975), p. 31.

88. *New York Times,* January 26, 1975, reported a Kyodo, Japanese news agency dispatch that Sun Chien was a worker in the port of Tientsin.

89. Donald Klein, "The State Council of the Cultural Revolution," *The China Quarterly,* no. 35 (July/September 1968), p. 85.

90. Ibid.

91. *Peking Review,* no. 7 (February 14, 1975), p. 8.

92. *Peking Review,* no. 11 (March 14, 1975), p. 5.

93. *Red Flag,* no. 2 (February 1975), p. 52.

94. *Peking Review,* no. 7 (February 14, 1975), p. 4.

95. Ibid., p. 5.

96. *Peking Review,* no. 10 (March 7, 1975), p. 6.

97. *Peking Review,* no. 14 (April 4, 1975), p. 8.

98. Ibid., pp. 6–8.

In searching for general theories and universal propositions, political scientists in the field of comparative governments have in recent years grossly overemphasized the similarities of divergent political systems to the extent that the differences among systems have been frequently overlooked. As a result, there are those who mistakenly believe that the political process in China is essentially identical to that in Western countries, and some have tried to interpret, analyze, and forecast China's political development using culture-bound concepts and theories, despite their limited relevance and usefulness.[1] This study offers an alternative approach by utilizing the notions of "faction" and "coalition" while taking into account the political and cultural characteristics that are also uniquely Chinese. However, analyzed here is nothing more than the tip of the proverbial iceberg of Chinese factionalism. Given the complexity and skillful camouflage surrounding Chinese politics, much remains to be done just to differentiate what is real from what is not; indeed, we know far too little at the present time to construct elaborate theories or fancy "models."[2]

## FACTIONS AND COALITIONS

As the Chinese Communists themselves have admitted, there are factions in China extending from the very top to the very bottom of the power structure, and, at every level, there are factions within factions. Though factions are determined on ideological grounds, coalitions are propagated as nonfactional arrangements. The "triple-alliance," for example, when first advocated, involved the participation of representatives of the military, cadres, and revolutionary rebels; in reality, however, none of these groups is an ideologically homogeneous body.

The military, for example, is not a monolithic, united force, which was amply demonstrated by their behavior during the Cultural Revolution. On the one hand, Lin Piao and his Fourth Field Army forces supported the leftists when Lin allied himself with the CCRG; on the other hand, Ch'en Tsai-tao, the Second Field Army commander of the Wuhan MR, fought on the side of the rightists. In both instances, there were dissident units that did not go along with the wishes of their commanders.

Cadres, too, are a divided group. Animosity exists between new cadres appointed during the Cultural Revolution and old "liberated" cadres victimized by the leftists. According to Wang Hung-wen, some old cadres could not "forget the attacks by the masses. Once liberated and in power, they seek every opportunity for revenge," saying "accounts should be settled," and considering themselves lenient for not retaliating with "interest."[3] Wang further claimed:

> Old cadres who made mistakes are allowed to make corrections. But new cadres will be clubbed to death as soon as they make a mistake.[4]

Factionalism among the mass representatives is the most notorious. Not only are they divided into worker and peasant units on the right and Red Guard groups on the left, but at the same time they are splintered into competing, antagonistic subfactions. The internal disharmony within the Red Guard groups, for example, was revealed by Chou En-lai:

> In most cases, revolutionary rebel groups disintegrated from the inside immediately after seizing power and divided themselves into two or three factions. This happened in many provinces. When the rebels seized power, they often did not seize power together as only one faction. The seizure of power by one faction cannot be called a success. The situation in Anhwei is an example. Two factions both opposed Li Pao-hua but only one faction seized power. One faction was called the "good" faction, and the other the "fart" faction. The faction which seized power said that it was very good; the other faction said, "good like fart." Yet both were on the same firing line together when suppressed in the past. Kiangsu is like this, too. There were two factions in Shansi, as well as Kwangtung, Kwangsi, Chekiang, and Fukien. Seizure in Heilungkiang was at first a collective undertaking, but the group soon divided into factions: one, the "mountain top" faction, and the other the "mountain bottom" faction. The problem in that province was solved when the two factions reached an agreement and received instructions from the Party Central.[5]

Anna Louise Strong also reported on the almost insuperable difficulties involved in trying to organize a Red Guard congress in Peking:

It was not easy to bring together into one unified organization the thousands of Red Guard groups which had sprung up spontaneously, always several and sometimes a hundred groups in one university and many of them fighting one another.[6]

When the "triple-alliance" was later modified to mean a coalition of "the old, the middle-aged, and the young," the ideological designations of "right," "left," and "middle" were still valid. For the most part, the old, whether in the Party or army, support the conservative cause, while the young are the most radical, identifying themselves with the leftists. Wang Hung-wen expressed the sentiment of the young when he said that he "always advocates the appointment of men in their thirties as commanders of large MRs."[7]

While difficult to prove that Chinese culture is faction prone, it is fair to say that factional politics have been a recurring, persistent phenomenon in Chinese history. However, it is easier to describe factionalism than explain its causes. One suspects that the intolerance of dissent in the political system could be a major contributing factor. In China, as elsewhere, it is unrealistic to assume that everyone agrees on crucial issues. So factions are formed, in the absence of other alternatives, to perform functions usually carried out by political parties in a democratic system, such as articulating ideological differences or competing for governmental control. But unlike political parties in the West, factions in China are essentially "informal groups"[8] without formal organization, prescribed constitution, or rules. Their memberships are flexible, shifting, and occasionally overlapping, depending upon the changing importance of the issue involved, even to the extent of absorbing former opponents or expelling previous allies.[9] Under the threat of persecution, factions resort to channels of communication that are most frequently covert and personal, a devious modus operandi that gives rise to cases of purposeful misinterpretation, feigned compliance, such as "waving the red flag to oppose the red flag," and innuendo, such as "pointing at the chicken but cursing the dog."

The growth of factions in the CCP can also be traced to the early stages of the Chinese Communist movement. In guerrilla days, local commanders and cadres by necessity had to function independently of the center and enjoyed varying degrees of autonomy. After liberation in 1949, China was unified and centralized rule was initiated. However, because of primitive transportation and communication systems and strong local sentiment, the "independent kingdoms" did not disappear but survived, though with substantially diminished powers and authority, particularly in the border regions.

Factions have also an origin in nepotism, widely practiced under the emperors and succeeding governments, whereby officials, high or low, attempt to obtain preferential treatment for members of their own families. At the national level, the wives of Mao, Lin Piao, and Chou En-lai have held high positions in the Party hierarchy at one time or another; Chiang Ch'ing, whose influence and stature skyrocketed during the Cultural Revolution, is the most conspicuous example. Children of leaders have also fared well in their respective careers. Yao Wen-yuan is widely rumored to be Mao's son-in-law;[10] Lin Li-kuo, Lin Piao's son, was a deputy minister of the air force before he presumably was killed in the 1972 air crash; and Wang Hai-jung, at present a vice-minister of the Ministry of Foreign Affairs, is the daughter of Mao's brother. Similar examples are too numerous to cite. This practice is even more widespread at local levels, although supporting evidence is extremely difficult to gather.

The "old-boy net,"[11] based on school ties, is also a contributing factor to the development of factions, particularly at lower levels. In China, as in many developing countries, the educated minority eventually becomes the governing elite, and the fact of having attended the same university or academy constitutes a solid foundation for mutual accommodation. One example would be the Anti-Japanese War College in Yenan, which has provided the locus for the "K'angta" faction, which occupies a disproportionately large number of command positions in the Chinese military.

Personal friendship and loyalty in a rural, agrarian, and tightly knit community typical of developing nations means a great deal more than it does in the more individualistic, industrialized, and impersonal societies of the West. Especially in China, these relationships are highly prized and play an important part in forming cliques that are often the components of a faction or subfaction.

In a highly factionalized political setting, coalitions are the most practical, and, in fact, the only way to gain power and control. The domination of one faction over all others provides the most durable alliance, but where two or more competing factions of roughly equal strength are involved, stability depends on a complex mix of diverse considerations. At the risk of oversimplification, it is possible to identify some of the most significant factors, such as the presence of a supreme leader who commands respect and obedience from both the ruling elite and the population; the availability of effective mediation; the absence of intensely felt disagreements over basic issues and policies, especially within the top leadership; the ability of the central authorities to demand faithful implementation of national policy; acceptance by all concerned of the "rules of the game" to resolve differences and conflicts; and, finally, the agreement not to involve the military or resort to the use of force.

## FUTURE PROSPECTS

In view of the scarcity and, in some cases, the uncertain quality of data so far available, it is exceedingly hazardous to make predictions regarding the future development of Chinese politics. As A. Doak Barnett so aptly phrased it, "The one thing that is certain about China is that one must expect the unexpected."[12] Nevertheless, it is possible to discern several major trends, if only in outline form, and to make some cautious speculations.

In the coming years, factionalism will persist. In fact, the Chinese Communists have said as much:

> Chairman Mao points out: "Apart from uninhabited deserts, wherever there are groups of people, they are invariably composed of the Left, the Middle, and the Right. This will still be the case after thousands of years." This is the truth.[13]

Coalitions, as constituted at present, do not augur well for stability in terms of the requirements mentioned earlier. As a means of unifying a heterogeneous population, the CCP meticulously cultivated the image and prestige of Mao to the extent that today he is revered "far more than Jesus Christ among the devout Christians in the West."[14] Particularly in the eyes of youth who are taught since childhood that "mother is dear and father is dear, but Chairman Mao is the dearest of them all," Mao is regarded as "the greatest genius of all time who knows everything and can do anything."[15] But while the cult of Mao has served the interests of the country well during his lifetime, a vacuum will occur upon Mao's death that cannot be filled by any other leader. So far, Chou En-lai has been able to mediate among the rival factions and, upon occasion, almost single-handedly saved China from total chaos and collapse, but it is uncertain whether he could muster the wholehearted support of the leftists in the event of Mao's death.

The central issue of right versus left splitting the top Party leadership continues to be the focus of contention, and the ability of Peking and Chou En-lai to elicit compliance from local leaders is questionable, despite the recent conclusion of the Fourth NPC which gave the impression of unity. Furthermore the "rules of the game" are by no means settled, even if they have been incorporated into the Party and state constitutions, which resemble statements of aspirations rather than concrete guidelines for policy. In the past, such documents have been ignored when convenient, and there is no reason to believe that the future will be different. Even on the question of the succession to Mao, no agreed-upon procedures are known to exist, and, if formulated, there is no assurance that they will be observed.

Finally, force remains now, as in the past, an integral part of Chinese politics. Even when the military is subordinate to the Party, as was the case before the Cultural Revolution and to a lesser degree today, those who "command the gun" constitute a potent group. As factional strife intensifies, participants will accelerate their cultivation and acquisition of military allies. Described as "kingmakers"[16] in the past, military leaders may yet play a decisive role if the country becomes again embroiled in a crisis caused by factional groups seeking supremacy after Mao's death.

All things considered, the factional struggle between the leftists and the rightists will continue unabated, reaching a climax on the momentous day that Mao Tse-tung dies. Indeed, it would be a miracle if factionalism in China became extinct and coalitions unnecessary in the years ahead.

## NOTES

1. Tang Tsou, "Comment," *The China Quarterly*, no. 65 (January-March 1976): 98–114.

2. See, for example, Andrew J. Nathan, "A Factionalism Model for CCP Politics," *The China Quarterly*, no. 53 (January-March 1973): 34–52.

3. "Wang Hung-wen's Report at the 'Central Study Class,' " *Chinese Communist Affairs Monthly 17*, no. 12 (February 1975): 84.

4. Ibid., p. 85.

5. Institute for the Study of Chinese Communist Problems, *Important CCP Documents of the Great Proletarian Cultural Revolution* (Taipei: Institute for the Study of Chinese Communist Problems, 1973), p. 256.

6. Anna Louise Strong, "Cultural Revolution at Beida," *Progressive Labor 6*, no. 2 (November-December 1967): 77; cited in Victor Nee, *The Cultural Revolution at Peking University* (New York: Monthly Review Press, 1969), p. 70.

7. "Wang Hung-wen's Report," op. cit., p. 80.

8. Tang, op. cit., p. 100.

9. Heath B. Chamberlain, "Limits of a One-Dimensional Approach," *Problems of Communism 24*, no. 1 (January-February 1975): 74.

10. For details, see Lynn T. White III, "Leadership in Shanghai, 1955–69," in *Elites in the People's Republic of China*, ed. Robert A. Scalapino (Seattle: University of Washington Press, 1972), p. 338, footnote 111.

11. William W. Whitson, "Comment," *The China Quarterly*, no. 57 (January-March 1974): 146.

12. A. Doak Barnett, *Uncertain Passage: China's Translation to the Post-Mao Era* (Washington, D.C.: Brookings Institution, 1974), p. xvi.

13. *Peking Review*, no. 19 (May 10, 1968): 3.

14. Ti Yü-kuei, "Why Did We Flee to Hong Kong?" *The China Monthly*, no. 714 (March 1, 1975): 24.

15. Ibid.

16. Parris H. Chang, "Regional Military Power: The Aftermath of the Cultural Revolution," *Asian Survey 12*, no. 12 (December 1972): 1012.

The early months of 1975 passed uneventfully like the lull in a storm. While Chou's health deteriorated, witnessed by his absence from all public appearances, Teng became the premier in everything but name. Ample evidence indicates that he exercised firm control over the country and continued to implement the moderate policies initiated by Chou. To return the government to civilian rule, the policy of reducing military dominance continued and the percentage of military personnel in civilian governing bodies steadily dropped. Only 12 of the 29 PPC first secretaries are military men, in contrast to the 22 earlier. A similar decrease occurred in the 29 RCs as well, where only 10 military leaders, as compared with 22 earlier, are chairmen. The corresponding rise in the percentage of cadres in these groups is dramatic: Among the 29 PPC first secretaries, cadres were increased from 7 to 17, and, among the RC chairmen, from 7 to 19 in 1975.[1]

Even more indicative of the return to pre-Cultural Revolution days was the increased rehabilitation of leaders purged earlier. Among the more than 100 so far pardoned, the most notable were Yang Ch'eng-wu; Yu Li-chin; Sung Jen–ch'iung; Chiang Nan-hsiang; Hsiao Hua; Liu Chih-chien; Fu Ch'ung-pi; and even Lo Jui-ching, who attended a July 31 reception celebrating the 48th anniversary of Army Day. More puzzling than Lo's return to public view was an NCNA release on the same day announcing the appointment of Wang Hung-wen, who had been spending many months in Shanghai, as the vice-chairman of the MAC. The next day, however, NCNA issued a correction, and Wang mysteriously lost his new title.[2]

The new emphasis on pragmatism and moderation was apparent in the economic sector as well for production, rather than revolution, received greater attention. On the whole, China's economy showed healthy progress, despite scattered reports of labor unrest. An especially violent incident happened in the city of Hangchow, where workers, on strike after being denied wage increases, "cut off water and electrical supplies, disrupted transportation, attacked local public security forces, committed murder and arson and looted state property."[3] Similar disturbances occurred in other cities in Chekiang as well as in other provinces, particularly Szechwan, but none were quite as serious.

In August 1975, the political scene was enlivened by the launching of a campaign to criticize the popular Chinese classic novel, *Water Margin*, which portrayed Sung Chiang, the folk hero, as a villain who masquerades as a rebel but is at heart a capitulationist. *Peking Review* reported:

> The history of our Party over the last 50 years or so proves that whoever practices revisionism practices capitulationism—class capitulationism in home affairs and national capitulationism in foreign affairs.[4]

For reasons that became clear only months later, it also repeated Mao's warning made at the height of the Cultural Revolution:

> Practice Marxism, and not revisionism; unite, and don't split; be open and aboveboard, and don't intrigue and conspire.[5]

In December, *Red Flag* published an article, "The Orientation of Educational Revolution Must Not Be Tampered With," revealing that a "strange theory" had recently spread among educational circles. The theory claimed that every change in revolutionary education since the Cultural Revolution was a "flop"; that the educational revolution had "gone too far and become a terrible mess"; and that its orientation should be "reversed."[6] This article particularly attacked the old "elitist" practice of recruiting university students directly from middle schools on the basis of their academic records. The poorly prepared children of the proletariat, vilified as "crude pottery on which no fine designs could be carved," were simply "flushed out"[7] and barred from universities, resulting in the creation of a "bourgeois intellectual aristocracy" mainly devoted to the cultivation of students who

> feel dizzy, pursue personal fame and gain. . . . Some, showing fear of hardship or death, did not take jobs assigned by the Party and the state, while others even degenerated into bourgeois rightists."[8]

According to this article, those who spread this "strange theory" were attempting "to reverse the verdict passed on the revisionist educational line" and "negate the great cultural revolution and change Chairman Mao's revolutionary line." The article further warned that "revisionism is still the main danger at present. The debate on the educational front is part of the struggle between the classes, two roads and two lines in society."[9]

On January 8, 1976, Chou En-lai died at the age of 78 after suffering from cancer since 1972.[10] Chou's death was a severe loss for Mao, a man of great vision but little ability to manage the day-to-day implementation of policies. Mao probably found Chou indispensable, particularly after the purge of so many experienced administrators and managers during the Cultural Revolution. It was an even greater loss for China because Chou's talents as a negotiator and mediator were desperately needed in a country torn by factional strife.

Within the top Party leadership, the terminal nature of his illness must have been known to many, and Chou probably prepared in every way possible for a smooth transfer of power to Teng Hsiao-p'ing, his personal choice as successor. Teng delivered the eulogy at Chou's funeral but then disappeared from public view, along with several other associates of Chou such as Yeh Chien-ying, Li Hsien-nien, Chou Jung-hsin, and Yu Ch'iu-li. No one at first viewed their disappearances as significant. It was assumed that they were occupied with a multitude of important matters requiring immediate attention after Chou's death.

The first sign that all was not well came on February 1, 1976, when *Red Flag* published a series of articles repeating the earlier charges that the controversy between right and left was still "very acute and complicated" because the results of the Cultural Revolution were "still not quite solid" and some places remained "in the grip of the bourgeoisie to this day."[11] Moreover, there were people in the field of education who "stirred up a Right-deviationist wind"[12] in an attempt to "destroy the fruits of the Great Proletarian Cultural Revolution," allowing the "bourgeoisie to exercise dictatorship over the proletariat."[13]

The February 6, 1976, editorial entitled "The Continuation and Deepening of the Great Proletarian Cultural Revolution" in *People's Daily* was less ambiguous in its attack, claiming that the "Right-deviationist wind" was organized by

> those capitalist-roaders who had been criticized and exposed during the Great Proletarian Cultural Revolution but have refused to show repentance. Some of them admitted defeat when the wind was blowing but started to reverse the verdicts immediately when the wind died down. Some had never admitted defeat. Among them, some are alien class elements who wormed their way into the revolutionary ranks and some were active during the period of democratic revolution but are antagonistic to the proletariat in everything in the socialist period.[14]

The next day, Hua Kuo-feng was appointed acting premier of the State Council and, in his official capacity, received the new Venezuelan ambassador together with the foreign minister, Ch'iao Kuan-hua.[15] Teng Hsiao-p'ing was not even mentioned in the press, and his future began to look perilous.

In the ensuing weeks, more concrete and specific issues, not merely "what Confucian maxims Lin Piao hung over his bed,"[16] were published by both *People's Daily* and *Red Flag* accusing "unrepentant capitalist-roaders" of "deceptively" putting forward, early in the spring of 1975, the slogan "taking the three instructions as the key link." These instructions are to study the theory of the dictatorship of the proletariat and combat and prevent revisionism; to maintain stability and unity; and to promote the national economy. Furthermore, they claimed these three instructions were "interrelated and cannot be separated from one another" and should be taken as "the general program for all kinds of work."[17]

Though Mao himself had given these three instructions "on different occasions and under different circumstances,"[18] to put the last two "on the same footing" with the first was to "emasculate" his instructions "in toto,"[19] as Mao himself explained later:

> Stability and unity do not mean writing off class struggle; class struggle is the key link and everything else hinges on it.[20]

Therefore, it was a "sheer fraud"[21] to put, as they did, the development of the national economy as the "key link" and to appear "most dedicated to the realization of the four modernizations (i.e., to modernize agriculture, industry, national defense, science and technology)" first proposed by Chou En-lai at the Fourth National People's Congress. Criticizing Party leadership for a "lack of expertise and enthusiasm," "those unrepentant capitalist-roaders" proposed that experts should be brought back to run factories. Disapproving of "putting proletarian politics in command," they said, "How can we arouse the enthusiasm of the masses without putting profit in command and material incentives?" Downgrading the importance of the masses, they argued that "workers, peasants and soldiers can be relied on in a relative sense," but actually, it was necessary to practice "control, coercion and suppression."[22] Discrediting the policy of "walking on two legs" and encouraging "servility to things big and foreign,"[23] they opposed the policy of self-reliance and "taking the initiative in one's own hands and relying on one's own effort."[24]

In their attempt to "negate the achievements of the Great Proletarian Cultural Revolution and to strangle socialist new things," these capitalist-roaders complained that "the present is not as good as the past." They recruited "hermits" and "those who have fallen into obscurity"[25] in places where they regained control, giving important offices to those who "are not afraid of being struck down a second time."[26] By attacking young cadres whose rapid promotions were described as coming up "in helicopters" rather than "step by step,"[27] they ignored the principle of the "three-in-one combination of the old, the middle-aged and the young" and the requirement Mao gave for his successors in a speech to an enlarged session of the Politburo on March 20, 1967.[28]

On February 29, *People's Daily* began to use "that unrepentant capitalist-roader," rather than the earlier term "those unrepentant capitalist-roaders," and the reference was clear as it continued:

> It is still a refurbished version of his past fallacy: "I don't care whether it is Marxism or revisionism, socialism or imperialism. A cat that catches mice is a good cat, no matter whether it is white or black."[29]

And on March 28, 1976, Mao reportedly said:

> This person does not grasp class struggle; he has never referred to this key link. Still his theme of "white cat, black cat," making no distinction between imperialism and Marxism.[30]

In China, the unexpected has become the norm, yet few were not shocked to learn about the riot at Tien An Men Square on April 5, 1976. Since foreign correspondents who ventured too near were "turned away, mobbed, or knocked to the ground, especially if they had cameras or recorders,"[31] the only account available comes from official sources, but it is, nontheless, startling.

The riot broke out early in the morning and lasted all day and into the evening. The crowd was estimated at 100,000 people, but "only a handful of bad elements" took part in the disruption and arson. Several official automobiles were turned over and set afire, including a fire engine. A number of soldiers on guard duty were beaten and injured, and their barracks were smashed and set ablaze. Wu Teh, chairman of the Peking RC, gave a speech urging the crowd to disperse and mentioned Teng Hsiao-p'ing by name, for the first time, as "the unrepentant capitalist-roader."[32]

What seems to have triggered the riot was the premature removal of wreaths commemorating Chou En-lai at the Ching Ming festival, the annual event for Chinese to honor their dead. Some were clearly used as instruments to criticize Mao and the leftists; one, for example, carried this message:

> Devils howl as we pour out our grief
> We weep but the wolves laugh.
> We spill our blood in memory of the hero;
> Raising our brows, we unsheath our swords.
> China is no longer the China of yore,
> And the people are no longer wrapped in sheer ignorance;
> Gone for good is Ch'in Shih Huang's feudal society.
> We believe in Marxism-Leninism;
> To hell with those scholars who emasculate Marxism-Leninism!
> What we want is genuine Marxism-Leninism.

For the sake of genuine Marxism-Leninism
We fear not shedding our blood and laying down our lives.
The day modernization in the four fields is realized
We will come back to offer libations and sacrifices.[33]

The references to Ch'in Shih Huang and "genuine Marxism-Leninism," first made by Lin Piao in his "571" Project to attack Mao's policies, were, of course, slanderous; and the sentence, "the day modernization in the four fields is realized," could be interpreted as "lauding" the revisionist line of Teng Hsiao-p'ing.

Though the riot was quickly squashed, pro-Teng sentiment did not subside immediately. For several days afterward, poems and wall posters were written praising Teng's accomplishments "to the great satisfaction of the people throughout the country"[34] and urging him to follow the example of Imre Nagy in the 1956 Hungarian uprising. There were also people who described "the recent so-called anti-Right-deviationist struggle" as "the act of a handful of careerists to reverse verdicts."[35] According to a later report, some even "surreptitiously plotted to write letters to the Party Central Committee demanding that Teng Hsiao-p'ing 'be the premier' " or "abetted Teng Hsiao-p'ing by extolling his counter-revolutionary revisionist line." Still others "conspired on the sly in an effort to back up the hooligans in creating disturbances" or "carried out activities in public, putting up reactionary slogans and poems and making reactionary speeches, wildly spouting counter-revolutionary venom."[36]

Acting on Mao's proposal, the Politburo, on April 7, 1976, "unanimously" agreed to dismiss Teng Hsiao-p'ing from his posts as vice-chairman of the CCP, to which he was elected at the Second Plenum of the Tenth Central Committee held three days after the Fourth NPC, and first vice-premier of the State Council, but allowed him to retain his Party membership "so as to see how he will behave in the future."[37] From that time onward, criticisms of Teng mounted sharply and became increasingly personal. Mao, who was praised for having "penetrating insight into everything,"[38] allegedly discovered early in 1975 that Teng was the "wire-puller" behind the "Right-deviationist wind" that culminated in the "counter-revolutionary political incident at Tien An Men Square."[39] Indeed, Teng was accused of breaking the promise he made during the Cultural Revolution to "mend his ways and turn over a new leaf" and "never reverse the verdict."[40] Even though Mao "saved him and gave him the chance to resume work," Teng did not "live up to Chairman Mao's education and help,"[41] for as soon as Teng regained power,

he threw off his disguise and, with hatred grown tenfold and frenzy increased a hundredfold, brought all his experience in counter-revolutionary political struggle into play, cooking up a programme, preparing public opinion and mounting an organized and planned attack on the Party, with the spearhead directed at our great leader Chairman Mao.[42]

Knowing that Mao Tse-tung could not attend the Fourth NPC, Teng Hsiao-p'ing purposely went ahead with the convention and took steps "to ensure his own promotion and the appointment to high positions of his followers."[43] Not only did Teng Hsiao-p'ing rehabilitate Lo Jui-ching in July 1975, he also tried to "liberate" P'eng Chen and T'ao Chu.[44] He arranged Wang Hung-wen's long absence from Peking in 1975 so that he could preside over Politburo meetings, a privilege that should be accorded to Wang as the second vice-chairman of the Central Committee when Mao was away and Chou too ill to attend. Wishing to monopolize control of the army, he suppressed the NCNA announcement of Wang's appointment as vice-chairman of the MAC in July 1975.[45] Condemned as the "arch criminal" who should be attacked and "chased by all like a rat running across the street,"[46] Teng was finally identified as the person who preached "servility to things foreign and the doctrine of trailing behind at a snail's pace,"[47] phrases used by the leftists to indicate their unhappiness with Teng's policies immediately after the Fourth NPC in early 1975.

On the day of Teng Hsiao-p'ing's dismissal, the Politburo, again acting upon the recommendation of Mao, "unanimously" agreed to appoint Hua Kuo-feng first vice-chairman of the CCP and premier of the State Council, positions held by Chou En-lai before his death. Hua's appointments conformed with neither Article 9 of the 1973 Party Constitution nor Article 17 of the 1975 State Constitution. The former stipulated that the plenary session of the Central Committee should elect the chairman and vice-chairmen (though it also stated ambiguously that the Politburo and its Standing Committee should exercise the functions and powers of the Central Committee when the CC was not in plenary session), while the latter empowered only the National People's Congress to appoint the premier. In fact, when thanking the Venezuelan ambassador who congratulated him on his appointment as acting premier, Hua himself said, "It would still have to be confirmed by the National People's Congress,"[48] which has not been convened as of mid-1976.

Hua's emergence as the number 2 man in China, a surprise to many, does not conflict with recent developments. The deaths of Tung Pi-wu and Chou En-lai have tipped the delicate balance of power in favor of the leftists in the Standing Committee of the Politburo and the Politburo itself. Among the leftists considered eligible to succeed Chou, Hua is probably the most acceptable to those in the "middle" and the military, who acquiesced to the inevitable but probably resisted vigorously the appointment of Chang Ch'un-ch'iao or Wang Hung-wen.

Nevertheless, the elevation of Hua is a triumph for the leftists and Chiang Ch'ing, whose important role in the succession crisis has been consistently underestimated in the West. People in China probably know much more than the sparse information that has slipped through the bamboo curtain; reportedly, what the rioters shouted at Tien An Men Square was not "down with Ch'in Shih Huang," but "we don't want another Empress Dowager."[49] Indeed, Chiang's pivotal importance today can be seen from a picture taken on April 26, 1976, in which she stood in the center of "leading comrades" of the Central Committee receiving 130 representatives of the worker-militia of the capital, police, garrison guards, and personnel from the Ministry of Public Security who "gloriously performed meritorious exploits"[50] in controlling rioters at Tien An Men Square. The "leading comrades" numbered no more than 13, and only Ch'en Hsi-lien and Su Chen-hua were not members of the left faction. It seems certain that the leftists now have the upper hand as long as Mao lives, since Mao has a personal interest in supporting them so as to ensure the eternalization of his "thought"; to prevent his "de-Stalinization" after death; and to provide for his wife, who, if deprived of position and power, might be ill treated by those who oppose him. It is difficult to believe that Mao, who once remarked that Marxism-Leninism is "less useful than shit,"[51] has become a blind ideologue as well as a "revolutionary romantic."

But will the leftists be able to maintain their superiority and control after Mao's death, which seems imminent? Military commanders, especially those at the regional and provincial levels, have reportedly opposed the purge of Teng,[53] and many, who may have adopted the attitude of "waiting for the dust to settle" for the time being, may not stand by if their vital interests are threatened or if the country is engulfed in chaos. Furthermore, as the leftists again try to implement radical policies associated with the "Three Red Banners" and the Cultural Revolution, will the masses, who earlier "slowed down" or "lay down" in passive resistance, change their materialistic outlook and selfishness to embrace a utopian ideology demanding sacrifice and dedication at all costs?

In commemoration of the tenth anniversary of the "May 16th Circular," *Peking Review* proclaimed in an article "The Great Cultural Revolution Will Shine For Ever":

> Today, capitalism and revisionism are declining like "a setting sun in the west wind." The clowns who go against the tide of history may have their own way for a time but will eventually be swept onto the garbage heap of history by the people.[54]

Unless the Maoists can make communism, in its unadulterated form, work for China, despite its failures elsewhere, they will have to face the strong, more than somewhat ironic possibility that, in the long run, they may turn out to be the real "clowns."

# NOTES

1. Institute for the Study of Chinese Communist Problems, *1975 Yearbook on Chinese Communism,* Vol. 2 (Taipei: Institute for the Study of Chinese Communist Problems, 1975), pp. 8–9, 26–27.

2. For details, see *The China Monthly,* no. 722 (November 1, 1975): 39.

3. "Decision Regarding the Problem in Chekiang," *Studies on Chinese Communism 10,* no. 4 (April 1976): 15.

4. *Peking Review,* no. 37 (September 12, 1975): 7.

5. Ibid.

6. *Red Flag,* no. 12 (1975), in *Survey of People's Republic of China Magazines,* no. 75–38 (December 24–31, 1975): 2.

7. Ibid., p. 4.

8. Ibid., p. 7.

9. Ibid., p. 11.

10. For details, see *Peking Review,* no. 3 (January 16, 1976) and no. 4 (January 23, 1976).

11. *Survey of People's Republic of China Magazines* no. 76–8 (February 23–March 1, 1976): 3.

12. Ibid., p. 2.

13. Ibid., p. 4.

14. *Survey of People's Republic of China Press,* no. 76–7 (February 17–20, 1976): 29–30.

15. *Peking Review,* no. 7 (February 13, 1976): 3.

16. *Far Eastern Economic Review 91,* no. 10 (March 5, 1976): 14.

17. *Survey of People's Republic of China Press,* no. 76–9 (March 1–5, 1976): 129.

18. *Peking Review,* no. 13 (March 26, 1976): 9.

19. *Survey of People's Republic of China Press,* no. 76–11 (March 15–19, 1976): 112.

20. *Survey of People's Republic of China Press,* no. 76–9 (March 1–5, 1976): 128.

21. *Peking Review,* no. 14 (April 2, 1976): 5.

22. *Survey of People's Republic of China Press,* no. 76–11 (March 15–19, 1976): 114.

23. *Peking Review,* no. 14 (April 2, 1976): 4.

24. *Survey of People's Republic of China Press,* no. 76–11 (March 15–19, 1976): 114.

25. *Survey of People's Republic of China Press,* no. 76–9 (March 1–5, 1976): 132.

26. *Survey of People's Republic of China Press,* no. 76–11 (March 15–19, 1976): 114.

27. Ibid.

28. According to Mao, the successors should be "determined people who are young, have little education, a firm attitude, and the political experience to take over the work." See *Long Live Mao Tse-tung's Thought,* vol. 1 (n.p., 1969), p. 637. For the English translation, see *Joint Publications Research Service,* no. 61269–2 (February 20, 1974): 377–78.

29. *Survey of People's Republic of China Press,* no. 76–11 (March 15–19, 1976): 111.

30. *Peking Review,* no. 14 (April 2, 1976): 5.

31. *Far Eastern Economic Review 92,* no. 16 (April 16, 1976): 8.

32. *Peking Review,* no. 15 (April 9, 1976): 4.

33. *China News Analysis,* no. 1039 (May 7, 1976): 7.

34. *Peking Review,* no. 15 (April 9, 1976): 5.

35. Ibid., p. 6.

36. *Peking Review,* no. 17 (April 23, 1976): 13.

37. *Peking Review,* no. 15 (April 9, 1976): 3.

38. *Peking Review,* no. 17 (April 23, 1976): 12.

39. *Peking Review,* no. 21 (May 21, 1976): 7.

40. *Peking Review,* no. 20 (May 14, 1976): 13.

41. Ibid.

42. *Peking Review,* no. 21 (May 21, 1976): 7.

43. *Far Eastern Economic Review 91,* no. 9 (February 27, 1976): 8.

44. Ibid.

45. Ibid.

46. *Peking Review,* no. 19 (May 7, 1976): 14.

47. *Peking Review,* no. 24 (June 11, 1976): 11.

48. *Far Eastern Economic Review 91,* no. 8 (February 20, 1976): 13.

49. *Far Eastern Economic Review 92,* no. 16 (April 16, 1976): 9.

50. *Peking Review,* no. 18 (April 30, 1976): 3.

51. Stuart R. Schram, *The Political Thought of Mao Tse-tung* (New York: Praeger, 1963), p. 179; cited in Edward E. Rice, *Mao's Way* (Berkeley: University of California Press, 1972), p. 342.

52. A. Doak Barnett, *China after Mao* (Princeton: Princeton University Press, 1967), p. 46.

53. *Far Eastern Economic Review 91,* no. 12 (March 19, 1976): 14.

54. *Peking Review,* no. 21 (May 21, 1976): 10.

Y. C. CHANG is Associate Professor of Political Science at the University of Delaware.

He has written on a variety of topics on contemporary China and is a contributor to a book on a comparative analysis of the state constitution of the People's Republic.

Educated both in China and the United States, he holds an M.A. from the University of Wisconsin and a Ph.D. from Northwestern University.

DEVIANCE AND SOCIAL CONTROL IN CHINESE SOCIETY
edited by Richard W. Wilson,
Sidney L. Greenblatt, and
Amy Auerbacher Wilson

CHINA AND JAPAN—EMERGING GLOBAL POWERS
Peter G. Mueller and Douglas A.
Ross

CHINA AND THE GREAT POWERS: Relations with the United States, the
Soviet Union, and Japan
edited by Francis O. Wilcox

CHINA AND SOUTHEAST ASIA: Peking's Relations with Revolutionary
Movements
Jay Taylor

SINO-AMERICAN DETENTE AND ITS POLICY IMPLICATIONS
edited by Gene T. Hsiao

COMMUNIST POLITICS IN NORTH KOREA
Ilpyong J. Kim